COMPLETE

★ ★ ★

IPA

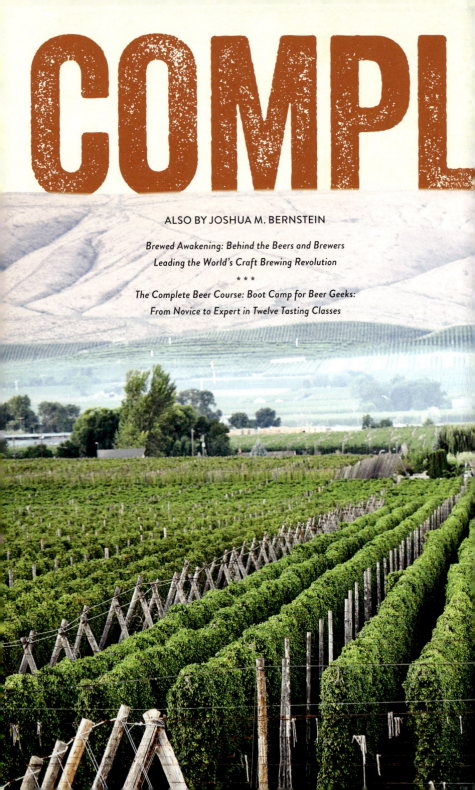

COMPL

ALSO BY JOSHUA M. BERNSTEIN

Brewed Awakening: Behind the Beers and Brewers
Leading the World's Craft Brewing Revolution

★ ★ ★

The Complete Beer Course: Boot Camp for Beer Geeks:
From Novice to Expert in Twelve Tasting Classes

ETE IPA

THE GUIDE TO YOUR FAVORITE CRAFT BEER

JOSHUA M. BERNSTEIN

STERLING EPICURE
New York

STERLING EPICURE
New York

An Imprint of Sterling Publishing Co., Inc.
1166 Avenue of the Americas
New York, NY 10036

Sterling Epicure is a trademark of Sterling Publishing Co., Inc.
The distinctive Sterling logo is a registered trademark of Sterling Publishing Co., Inc.

© 2016 by Joshua M. Bernstein

ISBN 978-1-4549-2072-4

Distributed in Canada by Sterling Publishing Co., Inc.
c/o Canadian Manda Group, 664 Annette Street
Toronto, Ontario, M6S 2C8, Canada
Distributed in the UK by GMC Distribution Services
Castle Place, 166 High Street, Lewes, East Sussex, BN7 1XU, UK
Distributed in Australia by NewSouth Books
45 Beach Street, Coogee, NSW 2034, Australia

For information about custom editions, special sales, and premium and corporate purchases, please contact Sterling Special Sales at 800-805-5489 or specialsales@sterlingpublishing.com.

Manufactured in Canada

2 4 6 8 10 9 7 5 3 1

www.sterlingpublishing.com

Interior design by Gavin Motnyk

Parts of this book appeared in different form in the following *Imbibe* articles written by the author: "Bitter Twist," "Feats of Strength," "Flavors: What to Drink in 2016," "Gold Standard," and "United States of Beer." The Brooklyn Brewery East IPA review was adapted from "Eastern Promise," published by *BeerAdvocate* magazine. The Sam Adams Rebel Raw review was adapted from "Sam Adams' Rebel Raw Is a Cult Beer for the Everyman," published by Eater.com.

For a complete list of image credits, see page 278.

To Jenene, for letting me fill our fridge, closets,
and cupboards with endlessly replenished IPAs.
I promise I'll do the recycling this weekend.

⚑ CONTENTS ⚑

4 ★ SESSION IPAS

PREFACE

Never doubt the power of a dollar bill. In the late 1990s, my wobbly undergrad days at Ohio University, I patronized O'Hooley's, a dark and smoky Irish brewpub that dispensed brown ales, pale ales, stouts, and other full-bodied crowd-pleasers. What made O'Hooley's special was Power Hour: For sixty glorious minutes, every house draft cost one dollar. A buck! At first, I downed three or four an hour, alcohol my chief concern. But over time, I started discussing the beers with friends, asking questions, divining why they tasted different. Those conversations led to monk-brewed Belgian tripels, robust barley wines, rich doppelbocks, and the occasional India pale ale—all more flavorful and interesting than anything glugged out of a party keg.

What a difference sixteen years can make. O'Hooley's has become the excellent Jackie O's Pub & Brewery, home to the Mystic Mama and Hop Ryot rye IPAs. Power Hour endures, though inflation means that non-imperial beers will set you back a whopping two dollars. Since my days there, the beer landscape has become an all-you-can-drink buffet, glutted with bourbon-barreled imperial stouts, salty 'n' sour German ales spritzed with blood oranges, and rustic saisons. But when people first approach that smorgasbord, glass in hand, they often reach for an IPA, the king of contemporary beer. It's today's introductory taste touchstone. Bitterness and citrus, pine trees and weedy dankness—those flavors and fragrances are easy to grasp, easy to love. A generation ago, brewing IPAs made brewers stand out. Now brewers make IPAs to fit in.

Nearly every brewer in America—more than 4,300 as I write, and climbing daily—and a growing number around the globe make some kind of IPA. The category is as elastic as it is overcrowded. Those three letters used to stand for bitterness and booze. Now IPA means flavor. It's anything and everything, a fever dream filled with hops, kegged, canned, bottled, and served cold.

As a journalist on the beer beat since the early Aughts, I spotted the uptick as IPAs grew brasher and more prevalent. Surely the wave would crest and crash, giving way to another, I thought. That's how trends work. Yet the IPA craze didn't move in a single surge; it became a rolling series of swells eroding the beachhead that beer equals fizzed-up yellow lager. To provide a concise snapshot of the pervasive, always changing style, I resolved to write *Complete IPA*. It's about beer, of course, but it's also about ingenious brewers transforming their raw materials into something distinct, memorable, and paradigm-shifting. That's no easy shakes.

Writing a book about the hurtling beer world can prove difficult. Setting aside the ground rule of one beer per brewery that I forced myself to obey, parts of the text might date before the book ever touches a shelf. I tried to read tea leaves, but with IPAs the only certainty is flux. There's likely some experimental hop, just taking root, filled with flavors we never dreamed possible, destined to upend the IPA game forever—and that's what keeps me writing and drinking (not necessarily in that order). We're living in an IPA world. Here's how to drink it, down to the dollar.

INTRODUCTION

Let's begin by shooting a hop-tipped arrow straight through the misshapen heart of a misconception. If you fancy IPAs, you no doubt have heard that they originated in the heady days of the British Empire. To safeguard their beers during long, hot, roiling voyages to India, brewers preserved their ales with elephantine amounts of hops. On the subcontinent, the bitter ales wet thirsty soldiers' whistles, becoming the swig of colonial India, then Britain, and eventually the world. Right?

False. It's the Tooth Fairy masquerading as truth.

Yes, bittered ale went to India, but so did the everyman's hop-rocked porter. Affluent Europeans, high-ranking officers, and civil servants all drank highly hopped pale ales, and huge hop charges were old news by then anyway. Brewers shipping beer to India and the Caribbean were hopping mad by the 1760s.

Pale ales appeared in the seventeenth century as the advent of kilns fueled by coke—a cleaner kind of coal—let maltsters produce paler malts. As the years poured on and exports intensified, so did hopping, leading to touts for "pale ale prepared for the East and West India climate." (Let's pause here to acknowledge a likely antecedent: October beer, an eighteenth-century favorite of the landed gentry. The pale, well-hopped beer was brewed in the fall, intended to mature on country estates for several years.)

Our tale really takes root in Burton-on-Trent, a small town in the West Midlands of England. Using the proceeds from selling his ale transportation business, William Bass established his eponymous brewery there in 1777. In time, Bass and other brewers earned a reputation for their Burton Pale Ale, strong, sweetish, and lighter than the prevailing brown ales and porters. Burton-on-Trent brewers did brisk trade with Russia and other Baltic

nations until 1822, when war and embargoes prompted Russia to ban British imports, including ale.

The brewers needed an economic lifeline, and the East India Company threw it to them. Among other goods, the EIC had been boating the hoppy pale ales made by George Hodgson's Bow Brewery of London to India. The arrangement worked just fine—until the money-hungry Hodgson puppet-mastered supply, creating fake shortages and fluctuating prices to undercut competition or increase profits. When Hodgson tried creating his own importing business, the EIC tapped Burton-on-Trent breweries to make the pale, bittered beer.

Affected by the area's plentiful gypsum deposits, Burton water's heightened levels of calcium and sulfates enhanced beer clarity, dried it out, and honed its bitterness. Bass, Allsopp, and other Burton brewers refined the mash bill, and around the 1840s East India pale ales marched headlong into history.

But that of course was just the beginning.

★ ★ ★

⬛ A SHORT HISTORY OF IPAS ⬛

The India pale ale—which reportedly first saw print in an 1835 issue of the *Liverpool Mercury*—had become big business overseas and, to a lesser extent, in Britain. (Domestic IPAs had lower hopping rates because brewers needed smaller preservative hop loads for intranational trips.) But the beer didn't leap to global domination. IPA's rise sits on the same timeline as the pilsner, the Czech lager that upended the way the world drank and nearly drove the IPA into the past.

Clear, crisp, and refreshing, the pilsner bubbled worldwide, but in Britain—according to Mitch Steele in his IPA treatise—the pilsner had a reputation for being a "ladies' drink." To compete, British brewers in the late 1800s started making lower-alcohol "running ales" served fresh and in casks brimming with live yeast. IPA popularity declined, hastened by ABV taxes and the temperance movement. As a result, the brewing recipe grew weaker and less lavishly hopped.

Stateside, though, prominent northeastern brewers—including C. H. Evans in New York's Hudson Valley; the Frank Jones Brewery in Portsmouth, New Hampshire; and Ballantine in Newark, New Jersey—continued the IPA tradition. They used Burton techniques, such as lengthy ripening in wood, and developed a domestic market . . . that Prohibition nearly obliterated. After the failed experiment ended, so did all the traditional IPA breweries, except Ballantine. They carried the IPA torch until 1972, when Falstaff Brewing bought Ballantine and dulled its IPA recipe. Pabst bought Falstaff in 1985 and discontinued the Ballantine IPA in 1996. (For more on the Ballantine revival, see page 43.)

When the American craft beer movement first fizzed to life in the late 1970s and early '80s, the landscape was brimming with cold, yellow lagers. To set themselves apart, Anchor Steam, Sierra Nevada, and other early independent breweries used the then-new Cascade hop—floral, citrusy, and unlike anything else. Anchor Liberty Ale and Sierra Nevada Pale Ale broke new gustatory ground (although rumor holds that Sierra Nevada's yeast strain descended from Ballantine yeast). Bitterness and flavor were taking root.

In 1989, the Great American Beer Festival awarded its first medals in the IPA category, and by the late 1990s IPAs became growth engines for brewers nationwide, from Portland, Oregon's BridgePort to Brooklyn Brewery. Newly developed hop varieties, such as the citrusy Centennial and the piney Simcoe, unlocked exhilarating realms of aroma and flavor. To curry attention, brewers sent ABV and IBU counts skyward in their double and triple IPAs. Experimentation didn't dead-end there. The unstoppable IPA now serves as an all-purpose flavor delivery vehicle, tweaked with wild yeast, heaped with wheat, filled with citrus, or aged in ex-bourbon barrels. Led by West Coast breweries, the bitter assault became a resounding triumph. According to research company IRI, IPA sales accounted for nearly 30 percent of the money spent on craft beer in 2015.

The onetime import has become an export. American-style IPAs are awakening taste buds in Buenos Aires, Barcelona, and Beijing. Hops, recipes, and brewing advice all lie within the click of a button. Beer trading allows IPAs to reach locales that normal distribution channels don't. Increased international travel brings drinkers to far-flung breweries, where a single sip can spark inspiration and a business plan. In this new beginning, brewers worldwide are molding the formula to suit their own climates and cultures. For example: Great Leap Brewing in China flavors their Ghost General Wheat IPA with Tsingtao Flower hops, while Italy's BrewFist suffuses its Space IPA with grape must. Malleable and ever-changing, the IPA has become a prize that can be created and re-created anywhere in the world, and it continues to spread like a fever that everyone wants to catch.

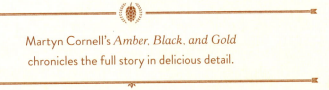

Martyn Cornell's *Amber, Black, and Gold* chronicles the full story in delicious detail.

⋗ OVERVIEW OF STYLES ⋖

ENGLISH IPA

The homegrown India pale ale thrives in two distinct worlds: established tradition and endless innovation. Meet Britain's most revered and buzziest IPAs, plus American brewers inspired by the time-tested template.

AMERICAN IPAS

The modern American IPA is chameleonic, taking on different tastes, aromas, and techniques from coast to coast. The bitter landscape contains seven distinct regions:

* Northeast and Mid-Atlantic: Juicy and fruity is all the rage, as a smooth, lush ride replaces the bitterness.

* Southeast: The heat makes southern brewers do strangely delicious things. Some create tropical fruit bombs, while others go resinous or embrace a substantial malt bill.

* Midwest: The heartland features many of America's foundational IPAs—balanced, not afraid to flaunt malt, but also embracing the latest and greatest hops.

* Rocky Mountains: If you favor IPAs that mimic marijuana in liquid form, hightail it to Colorado.

* Southwest: Hot days and cool nights conspire to create both drier and slightly more substantial IPAs that go gloriously overboard on aromatics rather than bitterness.

* West Coast: Potent bitterness and aroma fuel these lean, dry, and golden IPAs, turning them into high-powered performance vehicles.

* Pacific Northwest: Like pine trees and a citrus grove in liquid form, the slightly darker IPAs celebrate the agriculture-rich region's hop bounty.

DOUBLE & TRIPLE IPAS

By upping the alcohol level and adding mountains of hops, brewers are creating brash and aggressive, dank and resinous, or dangerously easy drinking beers. To eliminate unwanted sweetness, brewers commonly use dextrose, or corn sugar. Yeast easily devours these simple sugars, so the dextrose doesn't increase the body, creating a lighter, dryer beer.

SESSION IPA

Low in alcohol but full of flavor and bitterness, the session IPA has become the light beer of the twenty-first century.

EMERGING STYLES

Nothing stays static in the world of IPAs. New offshoots are appearing nearly every month. Behold, the most promising new IPA variants to try—right now, at least.

SEASONAL

* Wet & Fresh Hop IPAs: Green, vibrant, and fleeting, these harvest-season beers represent fall's finest.

GRAINS

* Wheat IPAs: Adding the grain to the brew kettle creates a smooth, cloudy sipper with a long-lasting head, a touch of tartness, and heady aromatics.

* Rye IPAs: As with whiskey, a bit of rye adds a peppery quality and a drying finish that invigorates taste buds.

COLORS

* Red IPAs: With a sweetness reminiscent of caramel or jam, red IPAs showcase today's fruit-forward hops.

* White IPAs: Borrowing from the Belgian witbier (wheat beer), these IPAs match spices to abundant hopping.

★ Black IPA: Also called a Cascadian dark ale or American black ale, the paradoxical style drinks dark and roasty with vibrant fragrant flourishes.

YEAST – DRIVEN

★ India Pale Lagers: By partnering lager's crispness with masses of citrusy, tropical, and piney hops, brewers have created clean refreshers with aromatics that pop.

★ Belgian IPAs: Popular on both sides of the pond, this style uses Belgian yeast to fruity, spicy perfection.

★ *Brettanomyces* IPAs: Wild yeast takes the IPA in dry and unexpected directions, from the tropics to the barnyard, and aging totally alters the liquid.

FLAVORED

★ Wood-Aged IPAs: By sending IPAs to nap in oak barrels that once held Chardonnay or bourbon, brewers are giving the drink enormous complexity.

★ Citrus, Vegetable & Spiced IPAs: Blood oranges, pink pepper, and even carrots are broadening what it means to make an IPA.

★ Coffee IPAs: This morning-night mash-up explores coffee beans' subtler, fruitier side.

SOUR & UNUSUAL

★ Dry-Hopped Sours: Infusing sour ale with hops creates a thirst quencher with beguiling new dimensions of aroma and flavor.

★ New Frontiers: From nitrogen infusion to dosing beers with cannabidiol (hemp extract), these IPAs take a trip to the exotic fringe.

⚞ HOPS ⚟

Hops didn't always have a stranglehold on beer. In the Middle Ages, beers derived their flavor from gruit (pronounced "grew-it" or "groot"), a proprietary grab bag of herbs, including bitter yarrow, wild rosemary, bog myrtle, and sundry spices. Gruit beer also doubled as an aphrodisiac and stimulant because brewers often added psychotropics. Henbane and nightshade for the trippy win!

By the 1700s, gruit largely had given way to hops, the female flowering cones of *Humulus lupulus*, a climbing plant from the same family as cannabis. Hops became the handyman of beer, boosting head retention, supplying bitterness to balance malt sweetness, adding flashy flavors and enticing aromas, and safeguarding against bacteria. If a beer is a car, grains are the chassis, yeast is the engine, and hops are the pulse-quickening, gotta-have-'em bells and whistles.

Hops don't grow on a vine. I repeat: Hops don't grow on a vine. They grow on a *bine*, a climbing plant that wraps itself around support structures, such as a trellis.

The Catholic Church controlled the gruit trade in the Middle Ages, levying taxes on brewers and the blended herbs.

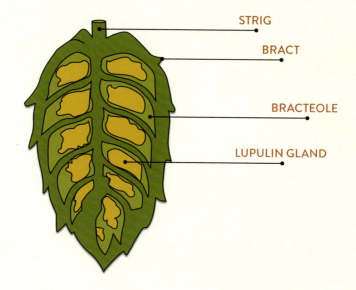

STRIG

BRACT

BRACTEOLE

LUPULIN GLAND

Strig: The central stem connects the flower to the bine.

Bract: The outer petals of the cone.

Bracteoles: The inner petals of the cone give the flower structure and protect the lupulin glands.

Lupulin Glands: These glands that look like yellow pollen produce the resin and essential oils that supply beer with its signature aroma and flavor.

Scientists have identified more than four hundred different compounds are in hop oil, allowing growers to play endless games of mix-and-match to create great new permutations of aroma and flavor. The four main compounds: myrcene, humulene, caryophyllene, and farnesene. Hop resins contain instrumental acids: The beta acids impart short-lived and lustworthy aroma. Alpha acids ensure preservation, their role shifting depending on where the hops go in the boil: early for bitterness, later and end stages for flavor and aroma.

Hops fall into two broad, sometimes overlapping categories:

Aroma: Flavor and aroma rather than bitterness characterize these hops that have high beta acids. To ensure that these fleeting, volatile aromas don't escape into the ether, brewers add them at the end of the boil and during dry-hopping.

Bittering: High in alpha acids, these hops primarily contribute bitterness rather than aroma or flavor and go into the boil earlier.

Hops thrive between the 35th and 50th parallels in both the northern and southern hemispheres, where abundant sunlight bathes summer days. They come from the same family as cannabis (Cannabaceae) and favor the same growing conditions as potatoes. In America, the majority of the country's hops grow in the Pacific Northwest. Washington's Yakima Valley accounts for some 75 percent of production. (Hop farms are sprouting across America, though, from Colorado to Wisconsin and Michigan to New York.) By weight, Germany is the world's largest hop-producing nation. Other key countries include Australia, Britain, Czechia, and New Zealand.

The hallmarks of pilsners and European lagers, noble hops are Czech and German varieties—including Hallertauer, Saaz, Spalt, and Tettnanger—prized for their spiciness, herbaceousness, and zest.

Hop bines typically sky to eighteen feet, but growers are experimenting with low-trellis (also called "dwarf" or "hedgerow") varieties. Advantages: less infrastructure, lower labor costs, and mobile picking machines that harvest the hops in the field. Disadvantage: lower yield.

Hop crops usually are harvested from late August through early October, when the bines are mechanically cut from trellises, whisked through picking and cleaning machines, and then to a kiln for drying to prevent spoilage.

HOP VARIETIES

Here are some of the world's most popular hop varieties, their flavor characteristics, and their primary usage in the brewing process. Dual-purpose means the hops contribute flavor and aroma as well as bitterness.

Ahtanum (USA) Fairly grapefruity and floral, alongside notes of pine and earth, with relatively low bitterness. Dual-purpose.

Amarillo (USA) Semisweet and super-citrusy, verging on oranges, like Cascade on steroids. Dual-purpose.

Apollo (USA) Potent notes of resin, spice, and citrus—mainly orange. Bittering.

Azacca (USA) Named after the Haitian god of agriculture, the dwarf hop offers a fruit basket of papayas, pineapples, lemons, and pears, with a touch of pine. Aroma.

Belma (USA) This Yakima Valley hop conjures oranges, with support from strawberries, pineapples, and melons. Dual-purpose.

Brewer's Gold (UK) Complex, pungent variety with a spicy aroma and flavor as well as a streak of black currant. Bittering.

Calypso (USA) has a fruity aroma that reveals pears and apples. Dual-purpose.

Cascade (USA) A floral hop that smells strongly of citrus, sometimes grapefruit. Dual-purpose.

Centennial (USA) Over-the-top citrus flavor and aroma with a relatively restrained floral nose. Dual-purpose.

Chinook (USA) Herbal, earthy, smoky, and piney with some citrus for fun. Dual-purpose.

Citra (USA) Heavy aromas of lychee, mango, papaya, and pineapple. A full-on fruit attack. Dual-purpose.

Columbus/Tomahawk (USA) Earthy and mildly spicy with subtle flavors of citrus, Dual-purpose.

"The increased involvement between brewers and hop breeders, and the overall rise in the number of brewers and the tastes and styles they bring, has led to an expanded library of desired flavor and aromas from hops."

—Tim Matthews, director of brewing operations, Oskar Blues

Crystal (USA) Floral and spicy, reminiscent of cinnamon and black pepper. Dual-purpose.

El Dorado (USA) Pears, watermelon candy, and tropical fruit. Dual-purpose.

Equinox (USA) Aromas of lemons, limes, papayas, green pepper, and apples. Dual-purpose.

Falconer's Flight (USA) Plenty of grapefruit, lemon, citrus, and tropical fruit. Dual-purpose.

Fuggles (UK) Earthy, fruity, and vegetal. Dual-purpose.

Galaxy (Aus) Citrus crossed with passion fruit. Dual-purpose.

Glacier (USA) Mellow with an agreeable fragrance that flits between gentle citrus and earth. Dual-purpose.

Goldings (UK) is called East Kent if grown in that region. Smooth and somewhat sweet flavor. Dual-purpose.

Green Bullet (NZ) Floral, resinous, and redolent of dark fruit. Nicely spicy, too. Dual-purpose.

Hallertau Blanc (EU) Grapes, grapefruit, passion fruit, pineapples, and lemongrass characterize this German hop's fragrance. Think white wine. Aroma.

Hallertauer (EU), one of Germany's noble hops, has a mild, agreeable perfume that's floral and earthy with some spice and fruit. Hallertauer encompasses several varieties; Hallertau often signifies hops grown in America. Dual-purpose.

Horizon (USA) Tidy and uncluttered, equal parts citric and floral with smooth bitterness. Dual-purpose.

Lemondrop (USA) Loads of fresh lemon, mixed with mint, green tea, and a little bit of melon. Aroma.

Liberty (USA) Mild, dignified aroma of herbs and earth. Dual-purpose.

Magnum (EU) Acutely spicy aroma conjures black pepper and perhaps nutmeg with a touch of citrus. Bittering.

"The most important process is making sure we select the choicest, dankest, most aromatic hops. Every year varies a little bit. Based on Mother Nature, maybe we get a little bit more tropical fruit, mango, melon, or guava characteristics."

—Matt Cole, brewmaster, Fat Head's Brewery

Mandarina Bavaria (EU) has a tangerine bouquet. Aroma.

Mosaic (USA) A montage of berries, tropical fruit, and citrus with an earthy, piney edge. Aroma.

Motueka (NZ) Lively, loaded with lemon, lime, and tropical fruit. Dual-purpose.

Mt. Hood (USA) Earthy and fresh with a restrained spicy nose that evokes noble hops. Aroma.

Nelson Sauvin (NZ) Partly named after the Sauvignon Blanc grape, bright, juicy, packed with passion fruit. Dual-purpose.

Nugget (USA) A bitter hop with a heavy herbal bouquet. Dual-purpose.

Pacific Gem (NZ) Gently reminiscent of berries and black pepper. Bittering.

Rakau (NZ) Ripe apricot and peaches as well as pine. Dual-purpose.

Riwaka (NZ) Grapefruit. Aroma.

Saaz (EU) A noble hop. Distinctly clean, cinnamon bouquet, typically used in pilsners. Dual-purpose.

Santiam (USA) Herbal, floral perfume that's reminiscent of a noble hop. Aroma.

Saphir (EU) Often used in pilsners and lagers, the German variety is finely spicy and fruity, reminiscent of tangerines. Aroma.

Simcoe (USA) Pine, wood, and citrus. Dual-purpose.

Sorachi Ace (USA) Japanese-bred hop with a strong lemony aroma that also suggests dill and can taste buttery. Aroma.

Sterling (USA) Spicy, sophisticated scent and assertive flavor. Dual-purpose.

Summit (USA) Up-front perfume of orange and tangerine. Bittering.

Target (UK) has an intense grassy, herbal, mineral character and a British floral scent. Bittering.

Topaz (Aus) contributes earthiness and a lychee fruitiness. Dual-purpose.

Vic Secret (Aus) Pineapple and passion fruit balanced by herbs and pine nuance. Originally known as Victoria's Secret. Aroma.

Waimea (NZ) Pine needles, tangerines, and pomelo. Dual-purpose.

Warrior (USA) Clean, smooth bitterness for hop-forward ales. Dual-purpose.

Willamette (USA) Herbal, earthy, and woody aroma with a little floral fruitiness. Dual-purpose.

A trend bubbling up from the homebrew ranks, SMASH (single malt and single hops) uses one grain and one hop variety so drinkers understand the individual characteristics of each ingredient.

HOPPING ALONG

If you've sipped an American pale ale or IPA in the last decade, the beer likely was brewed with C hops: Cascade, Centennial, Chinook, and Columbus. These American-grown cultivars pack the citrusy, piney, woody, and floral aromas and flavors that, when coupled with a bitter charge, define the contemporary IPA.

To stand apart, brewers need novel hops. Problem is, demand runs into the reality that hops require at least ten years to hit the market, so hop researchers must gaze into a crystal ball *and* cross their fingers. "I'm always joking that breeding is a pretty depressing job," says Jason Perrault, CEO and head breeder at Washington's Select Botanicals Group. "You're always looking for negatives." Strains can fall victim to mildew, produce low yields, or have unappealing flavors or scents. Which means ripping out the bines and starting over again.

"If we start with forty thousand seedlings and have one successful hop, then we are happy," Perrault says of the process, which includes extensive brewer trials. "If a hop breed is getting lukewarm interest from the brewer, it's not a good indicator. You need to have several brewers who are really interested in a hop to go forward." Not long ago, that prospect could prove challenging, such as when Select Botanicals released the piney, citrusy Simcoe in 2000. "It was a lot more difficult to get acceptance of a new aroma hop on a commercial scale," says Perrault. "It was like turning a big ship around in the ocean."

With the successes of Citra (2009), Mosaic (2012), and Equinox (2014), it's easier now to get brewers to take a chance on an original hop. Producing aroma hops geared toward American-style brewing has spread to international hop-breeding programs as well. The latest generation of hops coming from Germany, Australia, and New Zealand have plenty of citrus, tropical, and stone fruit notes but little pine or pungency. Hops are turning over yet another new leaf.

BREWING BEER IN TEN EASY STEPS

You didn't buy this book for a deep discourse on how grains, water, yeast, and hops foxtrot into happy hour, but here's a quick snapshot of the brewing process.

1. **Milling:** Crush grains—mostly barley malt and maybe rye or wheat—into grist.

2. **Mashing:** Heat water and steep grist in a big ol' vat. Starches convert into yeast-friendly fermentable sugars.

3. **Lautering:** Separate the sugar-rich liquid, called wort, from spent grain by running it through a lauter tun, a vessel with a slotted bottom. Hot water runs through the grains to extract lingering sugars, a process called sparging.

4. **Boiling:** Transfer the wort to a boil kettle, where the liquid simmers, with hops, for sterilization.

5. **Whirlpool:** Spin the hopped wort to separate it from sticky coagulated proteins and hop particulates called trub.

6. **Cooling:** Cool the wort to a yeast-friendly temperature by coursing it through a heat exchanger.

7. **Fermenting:** Move the wort to a shiny fermentation tank and add yeast.

8. **Conditioning:** When yeast cells gives up the ghost, they sink to the bottom of the fermentation tank, accelerated by cooling the vessels to around freezing. Then send the beer to a conditioning, or bright, tank for additional clarification, flavor development, and perhaps carbonation.

9. **Filtering:** To create crystal-clear clarity, some brewers filter the beers; others don't.

10. **Packaging:** Keg it, bottle it, or can it.

≡ ABVS ≡

Here are the average alcohol content levels of common IPAs.

3–5 PERCENT	5–7 PERCENT	6–8 PERCENT	8–10 PERCENT	10 PERCENT AND ABOVE
DRY-HOPPED SOURS	ENGLISH IPAS	BLACK IPAS	WOOD-AGED IPAS	TRIPLE IPAS
SESSION IPAS	WHEAT IPAS	INDIA PALE LAGERS	DOUBLE IPAS	QUADRUPLE IPAS
	WHITE IPAS	AMERICAN IPAS		
		RED IPAS		
		RYE IPAS		
		WILD IPAS		

≡ IBUS ≡

The International Bittering Units (IBU) scale calculates bitterness by measuring the presence of bittering compounds in a test sample. Alpha acids are water-insoluble, though. To unlock them, brewers simmer hops in wort, which turns the alpha acids into iso-alpha acids that drive beer's bitterness. The lower the IBU number, the less bitter something will taste; the higher the number, the more you'll need to say a palate prayer. Correct?

If only it were that simple. Let's say a 5 percent pale ale and a 7 percent IPA both boast 50 IBUs. Here's the problem: With less malt sweetness to mask the bite, the lower-alcohol beer will taste *more* bitter than the higher-alcohol brew. This is one reason that the beer reviews in this book don't give IBU measurements. Another reason: Everyone has a different bitterness sensitivity. Also, according to *The Oxford Companion to Beer*, the theoretical saturation point for iso-alpha acids in beer is 110 IBUs. (Higher IBUs have become an attention-grabbing point of pride for many breweries—even if the actual number doesn't come from rigorous science.) Nevertheless, buckle up and take a trip into IBU overload.

IBU EXAMPLE

40 | Ballast Point Even Keel Session IPA

45–50 | Firestone Walker Easy Jack

60 | Deschutes Fresh Squeezed IPA

65 | Founders Centennial IPA

73.5 | Smuttynose Finestkind IPA

77 | Stone IPA

82 | Uinta Hop Nosh IPA

85 | New Belgium Rampant Imperial IPA

102 | Avery Maharaja

112 | Founders Devil Dancer

114 | Short's Liberator

168 | Hoppin' Frog Mean Manalishi Double IPA

200+ | Airways Loud Lady IPA

225 | SingleCut Billy 200-Watt IIIPA

658 | Dogfish Head Hoo Lawd (IBU level corroborated by two separate labs—the highest count ever scientifically confirmed)

1,000 | Cerveceria Invicta

1,000 | Mikkeller 1000 IBU

1,100 | Triggerfish Kraken

2,500 | Flying Monkeys Alpha Fornication

⚌ GLASS ACT ⚌

It's no party foul to drink directly from bottle or can, but to appreciate beer fully it's best to pour it into a glass. Not all vessels are equal, though. The glassware symbols you'll find on the beer review pages refer to the below.

🍺 | **Nonic pint:** bulges toward the top to aid grip and to nix chipping. ("No nick," as the name goes.) Use it for session-strength brews to around the 8 percent threshold, when drinking by the pint becomes a woozy proposition. (The plain-slanted bar-standard shaker pint does nothing to enhance a beer's flavors or aromas, so skip it.)

🍷 | **Tulip glass:** named after the flower, ensnares aromas, and its flared lip helps preserve a handsome, lustrous head. Use it for Belgian beers, dry-hopped sours, high-ABV IPAs, and wild IPAs.

🍷 | **Snifter:** has a tapered contour that captures volatile aromas. Use it for triple IPAs and other brews that climb into the uppermost ABV echelons.

RECOMMENDED SERVING TEMPERATURES

COLD, 40–45°	COOL, 45–50°	CELLAR, 50–55°	WARM, 55–60°
INDIA PALE LAGER	FULL-STRENGTH IPA	BELGIAN IPA	WOOD-AGED IPA
SESSION IPAS	BLACK IPA	DRY-HOPPED SOUR	DOUBLE IPA
	CITRUS IPA	WILD IPA	TRIPLE IPA
	RED IPA		QUADRUPLE IPA
	RYE IPA		
	WHEAT IPA		
	WHITE IPA		

◄ A MATTER OF TASTE ►

We taste with more than just our mouths. To appreciate an IPA fully, tilt your glass to a 45-degree angle, and slowly pour the beer until the glass is half-full. While still pouring, slowly tilt the glass upright to make a foamy head. Foam is good! It captures the aromas that make IPAs so alluring. Now—

1. **Eyeball it.** Examine the color and clarity. Remember, looks don't always correlate with flavor. Dark IPAs can drink light, and unfiltered IPAs may taste better than clear ones.

2. **Swirl it.** Agitate the beer, and take a series of short and long sniffs. Repeat several times to decode the bouquet. Warmth can reveal new aromas, so try heating the glass with your hands. Then cover the glass with your palm and swirl again for a few seconds. Remove your hand, and inhale the concentrated aromatics.

3. **Sip it.** Pay attention as the liquid touches your lips, tongue, and throat as you taste. Does it feel light or heavy? Does the bitterness vanish or persist? After swallowing, take a breath, purse your lips, and exhale through your nose. (Aromas also rise from where your mouth and throat meet your nasal passage.) As your body heat warms the beer, note the different smell and taste notes.

Repeat—with another beer if needed. Practice makes perfect.

◄ THE MATCH GAME ►

Intense liquid bitterness can clash with food, but IPAs do go with certain foodstuffs. A caveat, though: No two IPAs are exactly alike, and finding a pairing that works for you might require a little work. That said, here are a few basic rules.

Fatty, salty, and fried foods subdue the IPA's bitter charge. Fried chicken, a juicy hamburger, creamy pasta, french fries, salty chips, crab cakes—you get the idea. A double IPA might overwhelm, so stick to session or standard strength. Try pairing a black IPA with a Cajun-style burger.

Mexican food, with its bright, herbal pop of cilantro, lime, chiles, and spicy chorizo, aligns nicely with session IPAs, especially those on the citrusy, tropical end of the spectrum. Avoid maltier IPAs, which can taste too sweet on the back end.

Fiery foods from India, Thailand, and the Caribbean often find common ground with IPAs, the bitterness helping to knock the heat down a notch. But beware boozy and rampantly bitter IPAs, which can magnify the perceived heat from vividly flavored and complexly spiced curries and other dishes.

Strong cheeses buddy up nicely with IPAs. A farmhouse-style or long-aged cheddar cozies up well with a standard IPA. A blue cheese (Gorgonzola, Roquefort, Stilton) can go toe-to-toe with an imperial IPA.

Sweet desserts also play well with hops. The jarringly delicious combo of carrot cake and IPAs has entered the pairing lexicon: The vegetable sweetness finds a toehold in the sweet malt as the sweet frosting modulates the bitterness. Skip the super-bitter IPAs, though, and go for one with some caramel nuance. A must-try: crème brûlée.

"One key thing fat does with IPA is protect the palate. If you practice the age-old order of tasting beer with food by going beer-food-beer, try reversing it and going food-beer-beer. The fat will hold hops back for a quick second, allowing malt to come through and complete the pairing. The trick with pairing IPA is to get the right amount of fat on the palate to stave off the initial hop attack, then go back for the second sip to get your full hop dose."

—Adam Dulye, executive chef of the Brewers Association

⊨ WHEN TO DRINK YOUR IPA ⊨

Fresh is best. An old IPA is a good IPA
—said no one ever—so drink up!

1

ENGLISH IPAS

Consider it a case of reverse colonization. During the 1980s and '90s, American brewers drew deeply from German, Belgian, and British recipe books to create euro-style beers. Hefeweizen caught folks' fancy, as well as witbiers, porters, stouts, and ales both pale and brown.

In time, the main muse became the IPA, molded with atypical malt bills and bittering regimens. The American offspring soon outshone its British sire, though, leaving the English IPA—biscuity and fruity, herbal-earthy and floral, not too boozy, sensibly bitter—preserved in amber. British beer has no shortage of traditions, but obeying ritual and convention hardly excites today's IPA drinkers. Old-guard Fuggles and Goldings hops rarely quicken pulses, and malt-balanced, lightly bitter IPAs don't make for an easy sell. To shake the status quo, UK brewers fighting the tide of bland, mass-market lager looked to America for new inspiration.

Scotland's BrewDog blazed the path with the finest Pacific Northwest hops, and, in the brick arches beneath railway viaducts, London soon reclaimed its heritage. Built in the early nineteenth century, these industrial spaces—now hosting restaurants, garages, and clubs—have filled increasingly with breweries, such as the Kernel, Brew by Numbers, and Fourpure. That quartet represents just a slice of one of the world's most exciting brewing scenes, where only delicious innovation unites them all.

🌾 CANNONBALL

MAGIC ROCK BREWING | ABV: 7.4%
HUDDERSFIELD, ENGLAND | AVAILABLE: YEAR-ROUND
MAGICROCKBREWING.COM | GLASS: 🍺 | BITTERNESS: ★★☆☆

Combine soft Yorkshire water with a love of American hops, and you'll start to understand Magic Rock, founded in 2011 by brothers Richard and Jonny Burhouse and named for their family's rock, crystal, and mineral wholesaling business. Head brewer Stuart Ross's ales charge headlong into a hop field, from the grassy Ringmaster and West Coast–inspired High Wire pale ales to Un-Human Cannonball, an annual triple IPA full of fresh American hops. The baseline Cannonball IPA offers a glorious explosion of peaches, mangos, and papayas stuck together with sweet resin. (Complete the trio by trying the Human Cannonball Double IPA, too.)

FUN FACT: Prodigiously bearded head brewer Stuart Ross won the Beard Liberation Front's 2015 Beard of Spring Award.

"We love San Diego–style IPAs and originally looked for intense hop aroma set against a very basic malt body and a dry finish. To maximize drinkability, IPAs should be really clean and belie their actual strength, so when a beer is 7 or 8 percent it should drink a couple of ABVs lower."

—Richard Burhouse, managing director, Magic Rock

⍽ HALCYON

THORNBRIDGE BREWERY | ABV: 7.4%

DERBYSHIRE, ENGLAND | AVAILABLE: YEAR-ROUND

THORNBRIDGEBREWERY.COM | GLASS: 🍺 | BITTERNESS: ★★☆☆

Born in 2005 in a stonemason's workshop on the grounds of Thornbridge Hall, a historic English country home, Thornbridge Brewery creates unpasteurized, unfiltered, uncompromising ales and lagers howling with flavor, ingenuity, and, yes, hops. Wild Raven, darkly fruity and evoking baker's chocolate, offers a paradigm of the style, and the balanced, citrus-focused, enduringly popular Jaipur—named for the city where Thornbridge Hall owners Jim and Emma Harrison wed—heralded a new UK IPA era. (Imperial-strength Jaipur X is a delicious doozy worth trying.) Their Colorado Red and Bear State brews nod heavily to American beer culture, but Halcyon looks to Australia. Galaxy and Topaz hops deliver richly tropical, berry goodness balanced by a sweetness reminiscent of honey-topped biscuits.

FUN FACT: Martin Dickie, who later cofounded BrewDog, codeveloped Jaipur IPA.

🌾 JACK HAMMER

BREWDOG | ABV: 7.2%

ABERDEEN, SCOTLAND | AVAILABLE: YEAR-ROUND

BREWDOG.COM | GLASS: 🍺 | BITTERNESS: ★★★★

Raising hackles and consumer expectations that a beer needn't taste like bubbly bathwater, BrewDog has altered the course of British brewing since Martin Dickie and James Watt founded it in 2007. Success goes to their signature blend of attention-grabbing exploits (bottles inside taxidermied squirrels, beers with ludicrously high ABVs) and brews flavored with a heavy hop load, including the tropical Punk IPA and imperial Hardcore IPA. Humming with more than 200 IBUs (theoretical, of course), Jack Hammer IPA features Centennial and Columbus hops driving an unrelenting bitterness. BrewDog also has a central Ohio brewery, so stateside drinkers can get a fresh whiff of Jack Hammer's great grapefruit aroma.

FUN FACT: BrewDog operates more than forty craft-focused bars in the UK and Europe, with locations in Barcelona, Brussels, Helsinki, and Rome.

The Spiegelau IPA glass, a collaboration between the German glass manufacturer and Sierra Nevada and Dogfish Head, has ridges and a laser-etched nucleation site that help aerate and enhance carbonation. It's fun to own but pretty fragile.

🌾 WHITE SHIELD

WORTHINGTON'S ALE | ABV: 5.6%

BURTON-ON-TRENT, ENGLAND | AVAILABLE: YEAR-ROUND

WORTHINGTONSALE.COM | GLASS: 🍺 | BITTERNESS: ★☆☆☆

In 1761, William Worthington founded his eponymous brewery in Burton-on-Trent. Calcium and sulfates that leached from local gypsum deposits into the water improved clarity and sharpened hop bitterness, leading to the modern pale ale and, *drum roll*, the India pale ale. According to legend, Worthington created its inaugural version of the incipient style in 1829. That hop-heavy beer, later renamed White Shield, stands as one of the world's longest-lived IPAs, brewed today in the historic National Brewery Centre. The bottle-conditioned White Shield is a full-bodied throwback, malt-forward, full of fruit and toffee, judiciously bitter and sweet. A classic, then as now.

For a deeper dive into Britain's brewing upheaval, read *Brew Britannia: The Strange Rebirth of British Beer* by Jessica Boak and Ray Bailey.

BREWERY FOCUS

THE KERNEL, LONDON, ENGLAND | THEKERNELBREWERY.COM

Stateside in 2007, on a consulting gig for Whole Foods, Irish cheesemonger Evin O'Riordain talked animals and pastures, aging and provenance, styles and flavors by day. By night, he joined colleagues at nearby d.b.a., one of Manhattan's best East Village beer bars. A Guinness man by birthright, he sipped and discussed pale ales and IPAs unlike any he had tried before. "Their intentionality to what they put into their mouths was exactly the same for beer as cheese was for me," he says.

Back in London, palate awakened, he sought American beers he'd enjoyed, but none tasted right. "Then the penny drops, and you go, 'Ah, you can't just import whatever you want, especially if it takes two or three months to get here.'" So he started homebrewing, helped found the London Amateur Brewers, and then went commercial by founding the Kernel.

By 2009 Scotland's BrewDog had cracked open the local IPA market, but only a handful of breweries were operating in London. Since then, from inside

a railroad arch in South London's Bermondsey district, the Kernel has become one of the UK's most vital breweries by showcasing hops in rarely replicated pale ales and IPAs served fresh and fragrant.

The Kernel's clean labels plainly describe beer style, hops used, alcohol content, bottling date, and that's it. "It can be a bit condescending to tell people what they're going to taste," O'Riordain says. Nor do they have a flagship beer or a single brewer. The dozen employees rotate tasks, including brewing, so "they're not just following the same recipe they brewed last week." Given Britain's predilection for lower ABVs, the Kernel's flyweight specialties include the tangy, lemony London Sour and Table Beer, essentially a session IPA treading around 3 percent. They also honor the past, brewing the historically accurate Imperial Brown Stout London 1856 and Export Stout London 1890, liquid history lessons and a tether to an era in which London beer ruled the world. "It's important for us to think of our place in a greater tradition," he says. "So much innovation is good, but we're all standing on the back of tradition that allows us to be here."

Ireland is issuing a swell of superb IPAs as well. Standouts: Galway Bay of Foam and Fury Double IPA, Kinnegar Black Bucket Black Rye IPA, and Eight Degrees Brewing's Nomad IPL and Hurricane IPA.

🌾 HADOUKEN

TINY REBEL BREWERY | ABV: 7.4%

NEWPORT, WALES | AVAILABLE: YEAR-ROUND

TINYREBEL.CO.UK | GLASS: 🍺 | BITTERNESS: ★★☆☆

Inspired by his grandfather's ginger beer, Welshman and trained electrician Gareth "Gazz" Williams started homebrewing in his twenties, a weekend hobby gone haywire that prompted him and brother-in-law Bradley Cummings to found Tiny Rebel in 2012. Their grassy Urban IPA, floral and spicy FUBAR pale ale (2014 Champion Beer of Wales), and Cwtch (pronounced "cutch," Welsh for "cuddle," and the 2015 Champion Beer of Britain) have buoyed their success. Hadouken, their "amplified IPA," contains a trio of American hops and has a tropical profile that doesn't taste like a fruit bomb, with pleasant sweetness and a drily bitter finish.

FUN FACT: In the *Street Fighter II* video game, Ryu shouts "Hadouken!" while emitting an energy pulse from his fists.

"For us, the hallmarks of a great IPA are perfect balance between malt, hops, and yeast, an IPA that says, 'I'll have another one of those!'"

—Gazz Williams, head brewer, Tiny Rebel

🌾 LIQUID MISTRESS

SIREN CRAFT BREW | ABV: 5.8%

WOKINGHAM, ENGLAND | AVAILABLE: YEAR-ROUND

SIRENCRAFTBREW.COM | GLASS: 🍺 | BITTERNESS: ★★☆☆

Wanting to focus on hop-forward American beers, Darron Anley founded Siren Craft, naming it for Greek myth's femme fatales who sang sailors to watery graves. He tapped American Ryan Witter-Merithew (now brewing at Hill Farmstead), who created a lineup that runs drinkers up the mast of intensity and flavor. Dive into Undercurrent, an oat-powered pale ale, before swimming over to Soundwave—a dry, West Coast–style IPA lively with grapefruit and peach—then backstroke to Calypso, a sour dry-hopped Berliner weisse. They also release a range of seasonal IPAs, brewed with rye, witbier yeast, and other rotating ingredients. Liquid Mistress, a red IPA, follows the West Coast mold, its sails full of citrus, caramel, and dried dark fruit.

To recreate Italy's Limoncello liqueur, Siren lightly soured the beer and added lemon zest and juice, lactose sugar, and tons of tropical Citra and lemony Sorachi Ace hops. They've also released Pompelmocello, made with grapefruit.

FULLER'S IPA

FULLER, SMITH & TURNER | ABV: 5.3%
LONDON, ENGLAND | AVAILABLE: YEAR-ROUND
FULLERS.CO.UK | GLASS: 🍺 | BITTERNESS: ★☆☆☆

Dating to 1845, Fuller's could coast easily on their heritage, brewing London Pride Pale Ale, London Porter, Vintage Ale, and ESB, but they don't rest on their laurels. Their American-inspired Montana Red brims with rye and passion-fruity Galaxy hops. They dry-hop their grapefruit-forward Wild River pale ale with Pacific Northwest varieties, and their floral Brit Hop, a cask specialty, features eight British-grown hops. They originally brewed Fuller's IPA, perched between old and new, for export. (In the UK, a variant is called Bengal Lancer.) The amber IPA is earthy, lightly floral, and herbal-spicy from the Fuggles, Goldings, and Target hop load. Well balanced, it has an ABV low enough that you can and should have more than one.

🌾 AXE EDGE

BUXTON BREWERY | ABV: 6.8%

BUXTON, ENGLAND | AVAILABLE: YEAR-ROUND

BUXTONBREWERY.CO.UK | GLASS: 🍺 | BITTERNESS: ★★★☆

The simple motto "Make better beer" guides Geoff Quinn's brewery, based in a spa town famed for its mineral-rich waters. Sample them at spring-fed St. Ann's Well or, better, in Buxton's character-crammed beers, such as the lime-tasting Wild Boar IPA, dry-hopped Berliner weisse Far Skyline, and Citra-enhanced SPA Pale Ale. Buxton's sharpest IPA is Axe Edge, named for a nearby elevation and laden with aroma-saturated Amarillo, Citra, and Nelson Sauvin hops, which make for a juicy celebration, fruit-sweet with a fat cap of creamy foam. If you dig imperial IPAs, look for the annual Double Axe.

FUN FACT: The structure on Buxton's labels is Solomon's Temple, aka Grinlow Tower. Built in 1896, supposedly to provide work for the unemployed, the tower is a "folly," designed to look old and with no practical purpose.

GREAT EASTERN IPA

REDCHURCH BREWERY | ABV: 7.4%

LONDON, ENGLAND | AVAILABLE: YEAR-ROUND

THEREDCHURCHBREWERY.COM | GLASS: 🍺 | BITTERNESS: ★★★☆

Deeply structured with rich, caramel malts and buzzing with Centennial, Chinook, and Columbus hops, the bittersweetness of the Great Eastern IPA brilliantly jostles with oranges, mangos, and pine. Redchurch's beer line also notably includes the session-weight Paradise Pale Ale and fruity Bethnal Pale Ale. Founders Tracy Cleland and Gary Ward, a TV producer and lawyer-turned-homebrewer, named their venture for the street where they lived in London's Bethnal Green district.

MEANTIME IPA

MEANTIME BREWING COMPANY | ABV: 7.4%
LONDON, ENGLAND | AVAILABLE: YEAR-ROUND
MEANTIMEBREWING.COM | GLASS: 🍷 | BITTERNESS: ★★☆☆

Part of the new generation reclaiming London's brewing heritage, Alastair Hook opened Meantime Brewing in 2000, but he never hooked his brewery to a single style, crafting classics, such as London Porter and London Stout, as well as newfangled creations, like the session-strength, citrusy Yakima Red. Made with Pacific Northwest hops and released in 2005 in corked and caged Champagne bottles (the first UK brewery to embrace the packaging), the IPA is utterly British, filled with native hops, including Fuggles and East Kent Goldings. Think caramel, toffee, biscuits, and tea mixed with moderate bitterness.

BREWERY SPOTLIGHT

RENAISSANCE BREWING COMPANY | BLENHEIM, NEW ZEALAND

To bring great beer to New Zealand's wine-washed Marlborough region, California natives, veteran brewers, and brothers-in-law Andy Deuchars and Brian Thiel founded Renaissance in 2005, fast finding fans for their English-inspired Perfection Pale Ale and fruity Discovery American Pale Ale, made with local Cascade and Willamette hops. Other noteworthy Renaissance brews include the Grandmaster Fresh Hop Double IPA and imperial-strength M.P.A. (Marlborough Pale Ale).

DRINK: Voyager IPA, inspired by bygone British beers and brewed with Fuggles and Riwaka hops.

⇒ ENGLISH-STYLE AMERICAN IPAS ⇐

During America's late-twentieth-century brewing revival, East Coast brew-ers in particular took inspiration from the UK. The British IPA template offered moderate bitterness, impeccable balance, a front-and-center malt profile, and earthier, fruitier hops. To that, they added a Stars-and-Stripes twist with American hops, nudging the bitterness northward.

By the early 2000s, these IPAs carried the torch of taste, as exemplified by Brooklyn East (India) IPA, Goose IPA, and Shipyard Fuggles. Then, as America's beer scene evolved, IPAs once considered fresh seemed out-dated. "English-style" came to mean fuddy-duddy as popular opinion ban-ished malt's sweet presence.

It's pointless to compare English-inspired American IPAs to Southern California's bright, citrusy, golden brews. They're cousins, yes, but they hang from distant branches of the family tree. Don't think of malt as a four-letter word, either; judge these IPAs on their own merits.

🌾 BALLANTINE IPA

PABST BREWING CO. | ABV: 7.2%

MILWAUKEE, WISCONSIN | AVAILABLE: YEAR-ROUND

BALLANTINEBEER.COM | GLASS: 🍺🍷 | BITTERNESS: ★★★☆

Born in 1840 in Newark, New Jersey, Ballantine had a glowing reputation for its IPA that aged in wooden vats for up to a year. Distilled hop oils and dry hopping supplied its assertive bitterness and penetrating aroma. Ballantine survived Prohibition, and in the 1950s the brewery ranked as the country's third largest. As the decades passed, though, Ballantine lost market share to rising light lagers. The mighty had fallen. Falstaff bought Ballantine, and Pabst bought Falstaff. A decade later, Pabst discontinued the brew, but in 2014 they relaunched it. "I began this project with a simple question: How would Peter Ballantine make his beer today?" said Pabst master brewer Gregory Deuhs of his research into devising a nineteenth-century beer brewed with twenty-first-century ingredients and techniques. Answer? It's sticky and resinous with a long-lasting head, crystalline sweetness, like an IPA crossbred with barley wine. A sipper for sure.

FUN FACT: From the 1940s through the 1960s, Ballantine sponsored the radio and TV broadcasts of New York Yankees games. Legendary announcer Mel Allen famously called Yankee home runs "Ballantine blasts."

🌾 GOOSE IPA

GOOSE ISLAND BEER COMPANY | ABV: 5.9%

CHICAGO, ILLINOIS | AVAILABLE: YEAR-ROUND

GOOSEISLAND.COM | GLASS: 🥛 | BITTERNESS: ★★☆☆

As Goose Island's head brewer in the late 1990s, Matt Brynildson (now brewmaster at Firestone Walker, page 228) decided to make a dry-hopped IPA indebted to West Coast beers like Sierra Nevada Celebration and Anchor Liberty Ale. Filled with American and European hops and supported by a pale malt base, Goose IPA originally was bottled, standard-style, with carbon dioxide. On draft, it was distributed nitrogenated, like Guinness. That bold move backfired, but the grapefruit-scented, earthily bitter, moderately strong, well-rounded brew has garnered half a dozen medals at the Great American Beer Festival since then.

Goose Island sources many of its hops from Idaho's Elk Mountain Hop Farm, also owned by AB InBev. One of America's largest hop farms, Elk Mountain grows Amarillo, Cascade, Mt. Hood, Saaz, and other varieties.

COMMODORE PERRY IPA

GREAT LAKES BREWING COMPANY | ABV: 7.7%

CLEVELAND, OHIO | AVAILABLE: YEAR-ROUND

GREATLAKESBREWING.COM | GLASS: 🍺 | BITTERNESS: ★★☆☆

In the Battle of Lake Erie, a key conflict of the War of 1812, Master Commandant Oliver Perry led U.S. Navy forces that defeated the British Royal Navy. Britain's loss has become an IPA drinker's gain. Great Lakes cooked up this English-inspired, tongue-in-cheek IPA that has stood as a Midwest classic for nearly twenty years. Perry brims with caramel, just the ballast it needs to withstand the volley of Willamette, Cascade, and Simcoe hops. Its fruit and pine taste profile will suit you just fine.

FUN FACT: Perry famously said, "Don't give up the ship!" The old label sported a playful spin on his phrase: "Don't give up the sip."

EAST IPA

BROOKLYN BREWERY | ABV: 6.9%

BROOKLYN, NEW YORK | AVAILABLE: YEAR-ROUND

BROOKLYNBREWERY.COM | GLASS: 🍺 | BITTERNESS: ★★☆☆

Introduced in 1995, this herbal, lightly piney, and floral East India Pale Ale recently shortened its name. Made with British malts and hops from the Pacific Northwest and the UK, this ocean-spanning beer echoes its nineteenth-century source of inspiration. "The name is a play on the original East India name, but we're also saying that we're proudly eastern," brewmaster Garrett Oliver says. "We're halfway between Yakima and East Kent, and our IPA reflects that."

FUN FACT: East IPA started as a summer seasonal before graduating to year-round status in 1996.

AMERICAN IPAS

In the early Aughts, IPAs had coastal affiliations: The East Coasters, indebted to England, ran darker, maltier, with citrusy or floral and earthy touches. West Coasters tasted dry, bitter, and bright, strongly scented with grapefruit, lemons, or mangos—an extra-boozy beach beer. Those classifications have shifted. Ohio, Scotland, and New Zealand alike brew West Coast–style IPAs today, and the once-maligned East Coast IPA has become hoppy, lustrous, soft, and typically unfiltered. Between the two coasts, brewers are developing regional IPAs every bit as distinct as BBQ. Southeast IPAs increasingly veer to tropical fruit; Rocky Mountain IPAs are turning dank and pungent; and Pacific Northwest IPAs often evoke pine trees drizzled with caramel.

Decades ago, beer styles arose from a confluence of geography, climate, ingredient access, and technology—or the lack thereof. Today everyone has access to the same ingredients and equipment, and stylistic tweaks spin the wheel forward, fresh and new. As it rolls along, new proponents climb aboard. So pack a pint glass and venture across the United States of Taste.

NORTHEAST & MID-ATLANTIC

Though balanced, malt-proud IPAs are still legion here, brewers are reinventing them. New York and points northward typically favor late-addition hops of the fruity and tropical sort, grains such as oats and wheat that impart a silky mouthfeel, and light filtration, resulting in juicy beers that look like a tall glass of orange juice—the bitterness all but banished.

⚜ LUNCH

MAINE BEER COMPANY | ABV: 7%

FREEPORT, MAINE | AVAILABLE: YEAR-ROUND

MAINEBEERCOMPANY.COM | GLASS: | BITTERNESS: ★★☆☆

Born in Portland, Maine Beer began as a pipsqueak outfit specializing in a single pale ale, Peeper, loaded with lemons and grapefruit but barely any bitterness. Since then, brothers Daniel and David Kleban have made flavor and fragrance Maine's calling card, most famously with Lunch. Named after a fin-nibbled whale, this IPA employs a hop quartet (Amarillo, Simcoe, Centennial, Warrior) to power a lip-smacker loaded with papayas, lemons, oranges, and pine. If you want their most coveted beer, the brewery-released Dinner, a twice dry-hopped double IPA, you'll have to line up with other fans in the early morning hours.

"We never set out to brew a beer based on regional trends. Our beers are uniquely 'Northeast' only in that we are located in Maine. We set out to brew hoppy beers that are balanced, clean, and packed with a tremendous amount of hop flavor and aroma, without being overly bitter."

—Daniel Kleban, cofounder, Maine Beer Co.

🌾 SUBSTANCE ALE

BISSELL BROTHERS | ABV: 6.6%

PORTLAND, MAINE | AVAILABLE: YEAR-ROUND

BISSELLBROTHERS.COM | GLASS: 🍺 | BITTERNESS: ★☆☆☆

After debuting their eponymous brewery in 2013, brothers Noah and Peter found a fast following for their contemporary approach to East Coast pale ales and IPAs. They focus on snowfall-smooth brews, heady aromatics, and bitterness as an accent rather than a roadblock. Canned by the pint, their Bucolia Amber Ale, Baby Genius Session IPA, and Swish Double IPA drink as easy as tap water. Substance smells like a Phish show, layered with lush flavors of citrus, pine needles, and tropical fruit. The bitterness calibrates the flavor rather than laying waste to it. The first taste will have you hooked.

If you dig Bissell's way smooth IPAs and find yourself near Philadelphia, visit Tired Hands Brewing Company, which focuses on farmhouse ales and hop-forward beers as soft as cashmere and juicier than ripe summer fruit. Drink their oat-filled HopHands Pale Ale and Alien Church.

IPA ITINERARY
⇒ MAINE ⇐

North Atlantic Ocean

For the latest info about Maine's breweries, visit mainebrewersguild.com.

DAY 1: YORK COUNTY

Crossing the state line, steer to Kittery's **BLACK BIRCH** Ⓐ (2 Government St., theblackbirch.com) for beer and comfort food. From there, canoe to **TRIBUTARY BREWING** Ⓑ (10 Shapleigh Rd., tributarybrewingcompany.com), and drink Tod Mott's well-balanced IPAs. Then make your way to **FUNKY BOW** Ⓒ (Ledgewood Ln., Lyman, funkybowbeercompany.com) to enjoy the weekend bands, wood-fired pizza, and the So Folkin' Hoppy and Jam Session IPAs before finishing at Biddeford's **BANDED HORN** Ⓓ (13-W, 32 Main St., banded horn.com), featuring specialties such as the Luminaire IPL; citrusy and sprucy Veridian IPA; and the fruity, resinous Daikaiju Double IPA. Reset your palate with the unfiltered Pepperell Pilsner, and call it a day.

DAY 2: PORTLAND

Start your trek in the Forest City at **RISING TIDE** Ⓔ (103 Fox St., risingtide brewing.com) with the Zephyr IPA or imperial Calcutta Cutter. Check out **BISSELL BROTHERS** Ⓕ (4 Thompson's Pt. #108-9, bissellbrothers.com), and sample their range from summer's Baby Genius Session IPA to the Swish Double IPA. Head to Industrial Way for Portland's densest collection of breweries. Start light at **AUSTIN STREET BREWERY** Ⓖ (1 Industrial Way #8, austinstreetbrewery.com) with the pine-laced, citrusy Patina Pale or the wild Brett Loves Hops IPA. Stroll to **FOUNDATION BREWING COMPANY** Ⓗ (1 Industrial Way #5, foundationbrew.com), for the juicy, oat-steered, smooth, and tropical Epiphany. Then cross the street to **ALLAGASH** Ⓘ (50 Industrial Way, allagash.com) for a Belgian-inspired beer, such as the spiced White.

DAY 3: CRUISE THE COAST

Head north to Freeport's **MAINE BEER COMPANY** Ⓙ (525 US-1, mainebeer company.com), a beloved IPA powerhouse that serves the piney, citrusy Weez and Another One, a roasty black ale and crisp IPA made with identical hops but different malts. Wind your way to Brunswick for **EBENEZER'S BREW PUB** Ⓚ (112 Pleasant St., no website) and its Lively Brewing outfit for the Mary Jane IPA and Dr. Dankenstein Double IPA. End your trip by cruising up Route 1, and pull into **MARSHALL WHARF BREWING** Ⓛ (40 Marshall Wharf, marshallwharf.com), which makes Big Twitch and the stronger, maltier Cant Dog Imperial IPA, then head for home.

🌾 CONGRESS STREET

TRILLIUM BREWING COMPANY | ABV: 7.2%

BOSTON, MASSACHUSETTS | AVAILABLE: YEAR-ROUND

TRILLIUMBREWING.COM | GLASS: 🍺 | BITTERNESS: ★★☆☆

Boston's beer scene is bursting with new stars like Trillium in the Fort Point neighborhood. Husband-and-wife team J. C. and Esther Tetreault focus on Belgian- and farmhouse-inspired beers, such as the strong and peppery Sunshower Saison, and pale ales and IPAs that taste flavorful, aromatic, and smooth. Fruity, citrusy Fort Point Pale Ale makes for a fine everyday sipper, but stock up on Congress Street IPA, a cloudy-golden ode to Australia's melony, peachy Galaxy hops. It's out of this world.

FUN FACT: Trillium's Stonington Saison ferments with wild yeast harvested from grape skins at the vineyard where the Tetreaults married.

When in Boston, also visit the venerable Cambridge Brewing (Belgian-style Audacity of Hops Double IPA, floral Flower Child) and up-and-coming Night Shift (soft and fruity Whirlpool Pale Ale, tropical Santilli IPA).

SUSAN

HILL FARMSTEAD BREWERY | ABV: 6.2%

GREENSBORO BEND, VERMONT | AVAILABLE: YEAR-ROUND

HILLFARMSTEAD.COM | GLASS: 🍺 | BITTERNESS: ★★☆☆

Off the beaten path in Vermont's bucolic Northeast Kingdom, Shaun Hill's brewery operates according to the *Field of Dreams* philosophy: If you brew it, they will come. RateBeer.com repeatedly anointed Hill Farmstead the world's best, and pilgrims flock here for growlers of the lavishly hopped, unfiltered ales that honor Hill's ancestors. Great-great-grandfather Ephraim is a resinous imperial IPA, great-grandfather Abner is a piney and citrusy double IPA, and grandpa Edward is a floral pale. Every beer offers a master class in flavor and restraint, especially cloudy-gold great-aunt Susan, which employs Citra, Simcoe, and New Zealand hops to create a succulent stew of lychees, grapefruit, peaches, and mangos rolled in pine resin.

When in Vermont, swing for doubles with Fiddlehead's Mastermind and Burlington Beer's It's Complicated Being a Wizard. Pop into Prohibition Pig for carnivorous vittles chased with the Alchemist's Focal Banger in Stowe. Then try Lost Nation's Mosaic IPA on your way to Hill Farmstead for whatever's fresh— in other words: everything.

🌾 GREEN

TREE HOUSE BREWING CO. | ABV: 7.5%

MONSON, MASSACHUSETTS | AVAILABLE: ROTATING

TREEEHOUSEBREW.COM | GLASS: 🍺 | BITTERNESS: ★☆☆☆

It seems like the more far-flung a brewery, the more drinkers will travel vast distances to wait in long lines for IPAs that often taste more like juice than beer. Can't blame 'em in this case. Founded in 2011 by a group of friends, including brewer Nate Lanier, Tree House specializes in fluffy, silky-smooth explorations of citrus and tropical fruit. The juicy beers pour like carbonated piña coladas. Julius contains a jolt of passion fruit and mango, while the Chinook hops in Sap conjure a Christmas tree. Made with gobs of Australian hops, Tree House's "cross-continental" Green tastes like sherbet made with lemons, oranges, and pineapples. As for the name, the first batch brimmed with so many hop particulates that the wort looked, well, you know.

🌾 FLOWER POWER

ITHACA BEER CO. | ABV: 7.5%

ITHACA, NEW YORK | AVAILABLE: YEAR-ROUND

ITHACABEER.COM | GLASS: 🍺 | BITTERNESS: ★★☆☆

To remain current, many breweries are reconfiguring IPAs with progressive hop varieties, intensifying aroma and flavor while minimizing bitterness. Such is the story of Ithaca's long-running Flower Power, which has undergone several reformulations from British-inspired to unabashedly floral. Today's honey-gold tweak—courtesy of Citra—has a medium body and tastes totally tropical, pelting your palate with tangerine, grapefruit, and pineapple. It also drinks pretty dang strong.

FUN FACT: Ithaca's former head brewer Jeff O'Neil now runs Hudson Valley's Industrial Arts, focusing on everyday-drinking, highly fragrant canned IPAs.

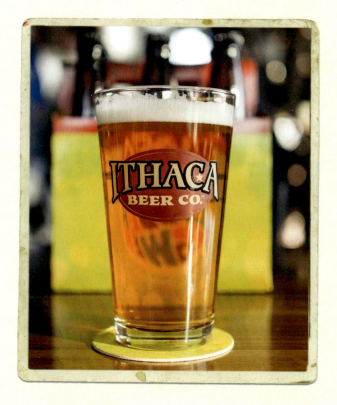

BREWERY FOCUS

STONEFACE BREWING COMPANY, NEWINGTON, NH | STONEFACEBREWING.COM

Peter Beauregard didn't care much for homebrew competitions. He and friend Erol Moe had been brewing for more than a decade but had entered only four or five contests, partly for impartial feedback on their ideal IPA: not too bitter or boozy, citrusy and slightly sweet. "We would get a medal every time we entered," Beauregard admits. "That was a bit eye-opening." But he never envisioned ditching his tech career until the Boston Homebrew Competition awarded top honors to their IPA. After that, "We said, 'Let's see if we can put pen to paper and get a brewery name.' "

A friend suggested Stoneface, referring to New Hampshire's Old Man of the Mountain rock formation, which had collapsed in 2003. The name had promise . . . and a potential trademark conflict with California's Stone Brewery. Stone cofounder Greg Koch didn't see any trouble, though, as long as Stoneface appeared as a single word. By 2014, they'd turned an auto-body shop into a commercial brewery specializing in burly imperial stouts and intense IPAs. "Those are the beers we like to drink," Beauregard says. They dry-hop their

Pale Ale—closest to their original homebrew recipe—with Falconer's Flight; Centennial and Citra make the IPA citrusy and tropical; and their Hopulization Double IPA tastes complexly fruity.

Instead of announcing their releases on social media far in advance, a common tactic in Vermont and Maine that draws in lines of drinkers, Stoneface prefers a low-wattage approach. "It's a difficult thing to manage," Beauregard says of dealing with lines. "I don't want people waiting outside in the snow for beer." He prefers the pleasure of walking inside the brewery and serendipitously finding a desired beer ready to grab. "It makes the beer accessible."

🌾 BE HOPPY

WORMTOWN BREWERY | ABV: 6.5%

WORCESTER, MASSACHUSETTS | AVAILABLE: YEAR-ROUND

WORMTOWNBREWERY.COM | GLASS: 🍺 | BITTERNESS: ★★★☆

Born in 2010 in the back of an ice cream shop and appropriating its hometown's nickname (coined by punk rockers), Wormtown has become the city's

biggest brewing success story. That happy triumph comes courtesy of Be Hoppy, their signature IPA. Unfiltered, generously dry-hopped, and the color of a summer sunset, it offers a floral whirl of grapefruit rind and lemon, the bitterness more emphatic than many northeastern IPAs. If you favor fruit over bitterness, try the slightly stronger Be Hoppier, which deploys Citra hops to great effect.

BREWERY SPOTLIGHT

GREAT LAKES BREWERY | TORONTO, CANADA 🇨🇦

Twice named brewery of the year at the Canadian Brewing Awards, Great Lakes has stood, since 1987, as a bulwark of Toronto's beer scene, and they've come a long way since the early days of malt-extract lagers. They've used their anything-goes Tank Ten series to test their Karma Citra IPA, muscularly bittered RoboHop Double IPA, Belgian-style Audrey Hopburn, and Octopus Wants to Fight IPA (eight hops, eight malts).

DRINK: THRUST!, a rocket blast of mangos and grapefruit.

☰ SOUTHEAST ☰

It took time for the Southeast to come to the IPA party, but the region is rapidly making its presence known with beers that evoke the ripe local bounty of tropical fruit, such as Creature Comforts' Tropicália. Others find their groove in blending rich malt bills to bright hops, both fruity and citrusy, or interpreting the West Coast IPA for local tastes.

⚭ PERNICIOUS

WICKED WEED BREWING | ABV: 7.3%
ASHEVILLE, NORTH CAROLINA | AVAILABLE: YEAR-ROUND
WICKEDWEEDBREWING.COM | GLASS: ▮ | BITTERNESS: ★★☆☆

King Henry VIII might have decreed hops a "pernicious and wicked weed," but this brewery celebrates the flowers' fragrant glory with pungent brawlers such as Freak of Nature Double IPA, blood orange–infused Hop Burglar, and Tyranny, a red ale romp through a Washington forest. (The brewery also excels at funked-up wild, sour, and barrel-aged potions.) At the 2015 Great American Beer Festival, Wicked Weed won silver for Pernicious, their flagship IPA that tastes like a lean, resinous, tropical love letter to the West Coast. "The idea of Pernicious stemmed from a conversation between me and my brother, Walt, on the flight back from 2014's Great American Beer Festival," says hop maestro Luke Dickinson. "We took a long look at what we thought the future flavors of Southeastern IPAs would be and concluded that, for us, it meant crafting a beer with huge mango and pineapple aromas supported by a soft bitterness and crisp, clean, and dry malt character. I couldn't be happier with this beer."

⚜ JAI ALAI IPA

CIGAR CITY BREWING | ABV: 7.5%
TAMPA, FLORIDA | AVAILABLE: YEAR-ROUND
CIGARCITYBREWING.COM | GLASS: 🍺 | BITTERNESS: ★★☆☆

Started in 2009 by Joey Redner, this brewery sinks guava into sour ales, crafts a brown ale modeled on a Cuban espresso, and creates a cucumber saison to slice through summer's swelter. Brewmaster Wayne Wambles has fashioned the copper-toned Jai Alai IPA (pronounced HI-lie and named for a Basque handball game popular in South Florida) to taste like a Sunshine State honeymoon, sticky with ripe papayas, mangos, and grove-fresh grapefruit. The smack of sweetness will keep you bouncing back for seconds.

Nearby St. Petersburg's buzziest brewery is Green Bench, which does well by farmhouse ales and IPAs such as the brightly tropical Sunshine City and tart, tropical Surrealist.

🌾 MONUMENTAL IPA

PORT CITY BREWING CO. | ABV: 6.3%

ALEXANDRIA, VIRGINIA | AVAILABLE: YEAR-ROUND

PORTCITYBREWING.COM | GLASS: 🍺 | BITTERNESS: ★★☆☆

At the 2015 Great American Beer Festival, judges named Port City the nation's small brewery of the year. The stylistically dexterous outfit also grabbed three medals at the fest: bronze for Optimal Wit, a Belgian-style witbier containing Virginia wheat; silver for a chocolaty, robust porter; and gold for the Monumental IPA, a coppery, citrusy-resinous riff on the classic East Coast IPA that celebrates flavors of toast and caramel instead of banishing them from the brew kettle.

FUN FACT: They use a Hopzooka, which blasts carbon dioxide to force hops into the beer without oxidizing it.

🌾 SWEETWATER IPA

SWEETWATER BREWING COMPANY | ABV: 6.3%
ATLANTA, GEORGIA | AVAILABLE: YEAR-ROUND
SWEETWATERBREW.COM | GLASS: 🍺 | BITTERNESS: ★★☆☆

After visiting Atlanta for the 1996 Summer Olympics, buddies Freddy Bensch and Kevin McNerney figured the ATL could use some West Coast–style hop aggression. Embracing "Don't float the mainstream" as its motto, SweetWater led with the grassy, citrusy 420 Extra Pale Ale, a flavorful revelation. Since then, the brewery has doubled down on hops with the Goin' Coastal pineapple IPA, Belgian-style Whiplash White IPA, and its namesake IPA. Unfiltered and heavily dry-hopped, the copper-gold citric and floral IPA packs a peck of pine and sweet caramel.

FUN FACT: In America, only Georgia and Mississippi ban breweries from selling beer directly to taproom visitors.

Head brewer Nick Nock experimented with hash—the gummy resin left after hops are ground and pelletized—in Johnny Hash, a double IPA that sold out double-quick. Now they use it in their Hash Session, Hop Hash Double, and Hash Brown IPAs.

BREWERY FOCUS

CREATURE COMFORTS BREWING CO., ATHENS, GEORGIA | CREATURECOMFORTSBEER.COM

In 2010, mysterious Creature Comforts IPAs suddenly appeared at dinners and events, bottle shares and bars, quickly building buzz. Not bad for a brewery that existed in David Stein's home. On the trek to go pro, Stein did a stint at Decatur's Brick Store Pub and an apprenticeship at Scotland's BrewDog and worked as head brewer at Twain's Billiards and Tap back in Georgia, where he refined a juicy IPA, low in bitterness and high in fruity aromatics and flavor.

Having honed his craft at Twain's, he opened Creature Comforts with Sweet-Water vet Adam Beauchamp in a 1940s Chevy dealership building in 2014. The duo use a rigorously scientific, restlessly creative approach to create high-quality, must-drink brews, such as rye ales aged in French oak with Ethiopian coffee, Berliner weisses flavored with guava and tart cherries, crisp pilsners, and, most prominently, IPAs embracing fruity pleasure and balance.

"We're taking inspiration from both the West Coast and the Northeast and creating a style that pulls from those but has a strong focus on being refreshing

and maybe a little more drinkable and approachable," Stein says. "Culturally in the South, we're really big on sweet tea. Plus, we have the whole 'It gets hot down here' thing."

Made with a calibrated blend of Citra, Centennial, and Galaxy, their Tropicália, a velveteen IPA waterlogged with ripe, heady flavors of mango, guava, and grapefruit, tastes like a tropical cruise to heaven. "We use hops that offer a fruity character, not fruit," Stein says. Tropicália has become their top seller, attracting drinkers once repelled by aggressive bitterness. "People often come up to me and tell me, 'I really don't like IPAs at all, but I like Tropicália,' " Stein says. "For me, that's the most rewarding thing about brewing."

⸙ HOP, DROP, 'N' ROLL

NODA BREWING COMPANY | ABV: 7.2%
CHARLOTTE, NORTH CAROLINA | AVAILABLE: YEAR-ROUND
NODABREWING.COM | GLASS: 🍺 | BITTERNESS: ★★☆☆

Starting in his garage, cofounder Todd Ford built a vibrantly brassy-gold beer and took a more-is-better approach to the hop bill, heaping on Amarillo and Citra to foster an IPA that's fruity and bready, piney and bright with sweet citrus. It's maltier than some might like but still a marvel. In 2014, the Queen City brewery—named after North Davidson, the main drag in the arts district—snagged gold at the World Beer Cup for its American-style IPA, leaping into the international limelight.

🌾 JADE

FOOTHILLS BREWING | ABV: 7.4%

WINSTON-SALEM, NORTH CAROLINA | AVAILABLE: YEAR-ROUND

FOOTHILLSBREWING.COM | GLASS: 🍺 | BITTERNESS: ★★☆☆

Jamie Bartholomaus started homebrewing in his college dorm room before founding Foothills in 2005, soon fashioning tasty delights such as Sexual Chocolate, an aphrodisiacal imperial stout; Torch, a Bohemian-style pilsner; the robust, espresso-licked People's Porter; and the nutty, tangerine-tinged Hoppyum IPA. The portfolio's bitter jewel is the Jade IPA, which takes its name from the herbal, citrusy New Zealand hops, accented by tropical Citra and piney Chinook. If you ever tire of this gem, look for their Hop of the Month beers that showcase the flavors of unique varietals, like New Zealand's lime-like Wakatu.

IPA ITINERARY
⚐ ASHEVILLE, NORTH CAROLINA ⚐

For the latest info about breweries in Asheville
and North Carolina, visit ncbeer.org.

DAY 1: SOUTH SLOPE

Start at **WICKED WEED BREWING**'s brewpub **A** (91 Biltmore Ave., wickedweed
brewing.com), where IPA-boiled peanuts pair perfectly with the resinous Pernicious
and Freak of Nature Double IPA, pungent with citrus and primo weed. Stroll to
TWIN LEAF B (144 Coxe Ave., twinleafbrewery.com) for the golden, juicy-fruity 144
IPA. Next, head to **GREEN MAN BREWING C** (27 Buxton Ave., greenmanbrewery
.com) for a rich, classic English-style IPA and Rainmaker Double IPA before
bopping to **BURIAL BEER D** (40 Collier Ave., burialbeer.com) to check out the
unforgettable mural while sipping the the Surf Wax, Skillet Donut Stout, and Scythe
Rye IPAs. Close the day at **WICKED WEED'S FUNKATORIUM E** (147 Coxe Ave.,
wickedweedbrewing.com) for a mouth-scrubbing, barrel-aged sour.

DAY 2: RIVER ARTS DISTRICT

Put down a BBQ layer, and begin at **WEDGE BREWING COMPANY** **F** (37 Paynes Way, wedgebrewing.com), situated in a former livestock distribution warehouse. Eyeball the sculptures while tasting the earthy, citrusy English-style Iron Rail IPA or Creature, a triple IPA by way of a Belgian tripel. Move on to **NEW BELGIUM** **G** (21 Craven St., newbelgium.com) for the tangerine-infused Citradelic IPA, bitter Ranger IPA, and the Rampant Imperial IPA. Then mosey to **OYSTER HOUSE BREWING COMPANY** **H** (625 Haywood Rd., oysterhousebeers.com), which serves IPAs agog with Galaxy and Mosaic hops alongside briny stouts seasoned with oysters.

DAY 3: SIERRA BLUES

At **TASTY BEVERAGE COMPANY** **I** (162 Coxe Ave., avl.tastybeverageco.com), pick up some bubbles for the road, and head east to **HIGHLAND BREWING** **J** (12 Old Charlotte Hwy, highlandbrewing.com) to pay homage to Oscar Wong, who catalyzed Asheville's brewing renaissance, by tasting the West Coast–style Highland IPA, heaped with Chinook and Citra, and the Devil's Britches Red IPA, named for a Great Smoky Mountains trail. Go south to Mills River, where **SIERRA NEVADA** **K** (100 Sierra Nevada Way, sierranevada.com) set up its first East Coast operation. Check out the stunning brewery grounds before hitting the taproom favorites, such as Torpedo and Hop Hunter, alongside experimental offerings, such as an IPA made with kölch yeast and German hops and a white IPA brewed with dwarf hops. Finish in Brevard, where **OSKAR BLUES** **L** (342 Mountain Industrial Dr., oskarblues.com) operates a Tar Heel outpost serving Pinner Session IPA, Deviant Dale's Double IPA, and the charged-up G'Knight Red IPA.

"We get first crack at some absolutely pristine water coming down from Black Mountain. Not too hard, not too soft . . . It's perfect water for beer," says Mike Rangel, who founded Asheville Brewing (77 Coxe Ave., ashevillebrewing.com), maker of the bitter Shiva IPA, then Two Moons Brew 'n' View.

HOPSECUTIONER IPA

TERRAPIN BEER CO. | ABV: 7.3%

ATHENS, GEORGIA | AVAILABLE: YEAR-ROUND

TERRAPINBEER.COM | GLASS: 🍺 | BITTERNESS: ★★☆☆

Seeking to make a hoppy beer for southern palates, brewmaster Spike Buckowski mixed up a pale ale recipe with citrusy and earthy hops and a grain bill incorporating 10 percent rye. Crisp and clean, the Rye Pale Ale became a galloping success. Terrapin has continued creating some of the South's most innovative, accessible, polished IPAs. Spring seasonal Mosaic features

its namesake in a red rye IPA; Hop Selection, an annual imperial IPA, contains a single varietal; and Hi-5 is as citrusy as they come. Hopsecutioner leans heavier on malt, with caramel under the hood and grapefruit and pine landing the aromatic death blow.

FUN FACT: In 2015, Terrapin partnered with *The Walking Dead* to create Blood Orange IPA, the official beer of the zombie apocalypse.

🌾 WESTBROOK IPA

WESTBROOK BREWING | ABV: 6.8%

MOUNT PLEASANT, SOUTH CAROLINA | AVAILABLE: YEAR-ROUND

WESTBROOKBREWING.COM | GLASS: 🍺 | BITTERNESS: ★★☆☆

South Carolina's beer landscape looked largely barren before husband and wife Ed and Morgan Westbrook opened their brewery in 2010, releasing convention-flouting conversation starters. They canned a salty-sour gose, spiked their Mexican Cake Imperial Stout with habaneros, and flung the White Thai Witbier to Southeast Asia with lemongrass and ginger. Sold in hop-green cans, the plainly named IPA is anything but. Festooned with fine, lingering foam and a rich, sturdily bitter flavor cut with grapefruit pith and an herbal edge, it's assertive without being overwhelming.

🌾 MISSILE IPA

CHAMPION BREWING COMPANY | ABV: 7%
CHARLOTTESVILLE, VIRGINIA | AVAILABLE: YEAR-ROUND
CHAMPIONBREWINGCOMPANY.COM | GLASS: 🍺 | BITTERNESS: ★★☆☆

Driven by DIY, punk-rock values, Champion underlines its name with mighty, mainstream-shirking, crushable beers. Killer Kölsch is a golden, grade-A refresher, while Shower Beer Pilsner encourages you to wet your whistle while you wash it. The production facility's nickname is "missile factory," and the Missile IPA starts with a pale malt base blasted with Summit, Simcoe, and Cascade. Its resinous bitterness lasts almost as long as teenage angst.

FUN FACT: Champion has created brews in conjunction with bands such as Against Me!, the Hold Steady, and pop punk progenitors NOFX, immortalized with the dank Stickin' in My Eye Rye IPA.

BREWERY SPOTLIGHT

LES BRASSEURS DU GRAND PARIS | LEVALLOIS-PERRET, FRANCE 🇫🇷

Bringing first-rate, American-inspired beers to France, Fabrice Le Goff and Anthony Baraff converted an office into My Beer Company, making citrusy pale ales, porters flavored with vanilla beans and cold-brew coffee, and other hallmarks of à la mode brewing. Expanded and renamed, Les Brasseurs du Grand Paris continues brewing IPAs such as the imperial Nice to Meet You!

DRINK: IPA Citra Galactique, filled with tropical Citra and fruity Galaxy hops.

⥽ MIDWEST ⥼

The heart of the country contains some of brewing's most bedrock-solid IPAs. Beers such as Founders Centennial IPA and Bell's Two Hearted Ale have inspired scores of beer makers. Balanced Midwest IPAs don't shirk from malt, but they also fragrantly showcase modern hops, favoring flavor and aroma over laying bitter waste to taste buds.

🌾 GONEAWAY

HALF ACRE BEER COMPANY | ABV: 7%

CHICAGO, ILLINOIS | AVAILABLE: FALL AND WINTER

HALFACREBEER.COM | GLASS: | BITTERNESS: ★★☆☆

"Hop genetics, growing, and usage are all evolving so rapidly. There will always be varietal-, aroma-, and malt body–driven IPAs and the alpha machines that pound bitter notes, but good brewers are pushing these elements into new places," says Gabriel Magliaro, founder of Half Acre Beer Company, Chicago's first brewery to can. Half Acre won silver at 2014's Great American Beer Festival for this punchy little number, then called Heyoka, a Lakota word that caused a kerfuffle. Half Acre changed the name to Senita, a southwestern cactus . . . until another brewery got litigious about brand confusion. Thus we arrive at GoneAway, a pale malt dream floating on a foggy orange boat sailing a happy medium between pine bitterness, tropical fruit, and an orange-grapefruit showdown.

When in Chicago, check out Pipeworks, fast building a name for its imperial stouts and creatively named and illustrated IPAs, such as the Ninja vs. Unicorn Double IPA and the Blood of the Unicorn hoppy red ale.

FURIOUS

SURLY BREWING CO. | ABV: 6.2%

MINNEAPOLIS, MINNESOTA | AVAILABLE: YEAR-ROUND

SURLYBREWING.COM | GLASS: 🍺 | BITTERNESS: ★★★☆

In 2004, obsessive homebrewer Omar Ansari went pro, installing a modest three-barrel system in his parents' former sandpaper factory. Two years later, Surly delivered the richly amber Furious, a British extra special bitter blended with an American IPA, consisting of Golden Promise malt, English ale yeast, and mounds of thoroughly American hops. The atypical mix became an instant hit, its caramel sweetness met by citrus rind and spruce, the bitterness as enduring as a Minnesota winter. A decade on, Furious remains their bestseller.

FUN FACT: Head brewer Todd Haug plays guitar for speed metal band Powermad.

Ansari championed legislation enabling Minnesota breweries to sell beer directly to consumers, paving the path for Surly to convert a potato-processing plant into a $20 million destination brewery featuring the Brewer's Table, one of America's only beer-exclusive fine-dining restaurants.

🌾 TRUTH

RHINEGEIST | ABV: 7.2%

CINCINNATI, OHIO | AVAILABLE: YEAR-ROUND

RHINEGEIST.COM | GLASS: 🍺 | BITTERNESS: ★★☆☆

So many German immigrants flooded into Cincinnati before Prohibition that the brewing district earned the nickname Over-the-Rhine. Reviving that tradition, Rhinegeist ("ghost of the Rhine") commandeered the abandoned Christian Moerlein Brewing Company bottling plant, turning it into a modern showcase for vivid, West Coast–inspired brews, such as the zesty Zen Pale Ale, tropical Pure Fury Pale Ale, and papaya-scented Saber Tooth Tiger Imperial IPA. Truth, an amber-orange dreamboat, tastes of papaya, passion fruit, and grapefruit from Centennial, Simcoe, Citra, and Amarillo hops.

Cross the Ohio River into Bellevue, Kentucky, and check out Party Source, a superstore of inebriation featuring an on-site bar and brewery, Ei8ht Ball, and New Riff, the distillery next door.

TWO HEARTED ALE

BELL'S BEER | ABV: 7%

KALAMAZOO, MICHIGAN | AVAILABLE: YEAR-ROUND

BELLSBEER.COM | GLASS: ▮ | BITTERNESS: ★★☆☆

Named after a Michigan trout river immortalized by Hemingway, Bell's flagship IPA stems from a 1993 homebrew experiment by Rik Dellinger and Rob Skalla. Using then-novel Centennial hops, they formulated a grapefruit-forward, pine-spritzed IPA that evolved into Two Hearted. At the time, it offered a taste bud–awakening trip into a flavorful new world, a land where malt balance and aggression shook hands and whispered: *You've found your new best drinking buddy*.

In the dead of winter, Bell's releases Hopslam, a highly anticipated double IPA devastatingly dry-hopped with Simcoe and balanced with a spoonful of honey.

🌾 WHITE RAJAH

THE BREW KETTLE | ABV: 6.8%

STRONGSVILLE, OHIO | AVAILABLE: YEAR-ROUND

THEBREWKETTLE.COM | GLASS: 🍺 | BITTERNESS: ★★☆☆

Brew Kettle began in 1995 as a brew-on-premise facility where amateur beer magicians could cook up their batches, then bottle their creations. The facility also operated a rinky-dink brewery, then known as Ringneck, which has grown into one of the belles of America's hops ball with fragrant pale ales like 4 C's and Old 21 Imperial IPA. The pick of the pack, though, is White Rajah, a flavor bomb of guava, peach, pineapple, and every Florida citrus under the sun. (Black Rajah is also worth belly space.)

🌾 ANTI-HERO IPA

REVOLUTION BREWING | ABV: 6.5%

CHICAGO, ILLINOIS | AVAILABLE: YEAR-ROUND

REVBREW.COM | GLASS: 🍺 | BITTERNESS: ★★☆☆

Nearly a decade after he selected a name and commissioned a logo, founder Josh Deth finally opened Revolution. His dream brewery has become a Chicago institution, many of the beers honoring uprisings and activists like Eugene Debs, who led 1894's crippling Pullman Railroad strike and whose likeness adorns the Eugene Porter

can. Anti-Hero IPA, "an American hop assault for all the ambivalent warriors who get the girl in the end," tastes less intense than that description suggests. It's a copper-gold charge that's floral and citric, with bitterness that'll keep you on your toes but not knock you down. While you're at it, look for other releases in the Hero IPA series, including the Jukebox Black IPA and Local, featuring Michigan-grown hops.

FUN FACT: The 2013 movie *Drinking Buddies*, starring Ron Livingston and Anna Kendrick, was filmed at Revolution.

BREWERY FOCUS

SPITEFUL BREWING, CHICAGO, ILLINOIS | SPITEFULBREWING.COM

Many breweries start small—in garages and other industrial nooks and crannies—initially capable of pumping out just two or three barrels, and hope that one glorious day the hard work will pay off. Less common is starting in quarters so tight that the equipment must be custom-made to fit for a rolling swap. "We couldn't brew and package at the same time," says Jason Stein, who cofounded Spiteful with friend Brad Shaffer in 2012. "We packaged Monday and Tuesday, then brewed Wednesday, Thursday, Friday."

From small spaces come big ideas. What Spiteful lacked in quantity, the brewery compensated for with dizzying variety and quality, including the humbly bitter Spiteful IPA, tropical Water Cooler Dictator Double IPA, hop-free Prove It Gruit, saisons aged in absinthe barrels, and the G.F.Y. Imperial Stout.

"Everyone always has a little spite in them," says Klein, who met Shaffer playing hockey in Chicago's suburbs. "Life is not just all sunshine or roses."

After returning from college, the friends disliked their day jobs and craved another career path. Opening a bar cost too much, so in 2009 they started

homebrewing, three batches a week for three years. Shaffer interned at IPA upstart Pipeworks, and "we essentially rented what amounts to a parking space in Chicago," Klein says. Lacking a taproom, Spiteful focused on packaging and distribution. "There's nothing worse than a double IPA sitting there without a label."

Because the brewery initially bottled only 22-ounce bombers, a pricier format associated with stronger beers, they focused on double IPAs and stouts. Expanding into cans allowed Spiteful to widen its IPA embrace, aiming for the moderate end of the IBU spectrum, finishing dry, bursting with hop aroma and flavor. Like many Midwest breweries, they're not afraid to use malt, with British Maris Otter punching the clock in Working for the Weekend. "It gives this nice, biscuity roundness without being too malty," Klein says.

Spiteful has upsized its equipment and space, but they still have their original kettle, and they still brew fun stuff, such as the lactose-infused You Don't Win Friends with Salad IPA or the God Damn Peanut Butter and Jelly Pigeon Porter among their four year-round staples: a pale ale, IPA, double IPA, and hoppy porter. "We definitely like our hops," Klein says spitelessly.

SCHLAFLY TASMANIAN IPA

SAINT LOUIS BREWERY | ABV: 7.2%

ST. LOUIS, MISSOURI | AVAILABLE: OCTOBER–FEBRUARY

SCHLAFLY.COM | GLASS: 🍺 | BITTERNESS: ★★☆☆

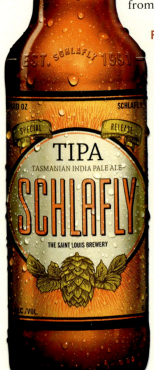

As IPAs have gone global, international brewers are clamoring for Pacific Northwest hops, crimping supply and pressing brewers to look elsewhere, such as Australia. Brewing under the Schlafly name since 1991, Saint Louis tackles two Aussie hops, Galaxy and Topaz, in its Tasmanian IPA. The result is a gorgeous, golden-orange beer that's lightly hazy with a fat white head. The fruit-sweet scent of Hawaiian pineapple with squeezes of lemons and limes follows through from first sip to last.

FUN FACT: To finance Saint Louis Brewery, Tom Schlafly borrowed money by using Anheuser-Busch stock as collateral.

🌾 MASALA MAMA IPA

TOWN HALL BREWERY | ABV: 6.5%

MINNEAPOLIS, MINNESOTA | AVAILABLE: YEAR-ROUND

TOWNHALLBREWERY.COM | GLASS: 🍺 | BITTERNESS: ★★☆☆

Many brewpubs established in the 1990s followed a pint-by-numbers pattern by brewing safe, color-coded crowd-pleasers—red ale, blondes, inky stouts—and pairing them with burgers, fries, and buckets of wings. Town Hall, which opened in 1997, has long shirked the status quo, turning out medal-nabbing provocations like the herbal LSD (lavender, sunflower honey, dates), Russian Roulette Chocolate Imperial Stout, and 1800 Old English IPA. The brisk bitterness of the far more contemporary, crimson-gold Masala Mama butts heads with jammy sweetness, citrus zest, light pine, and tropical fruit.

BREWERY SPOTLIGHT

AMAGER BRYGHUS | KASTRUP, DENMARK 🇩🇰

Homebrewing friends Morten Valentin Lundsbak and Jacob Storm founded Amager in 2007, naming it for its island locale and building it inside an air-raid shelter. Their Sinner series features the West Coast–style Envy IPA and Gluttony Double IPA, while top-shelf collaborations include the zesty Orange Crush IPA made with Cigar City and the Hill Farmstead–assisted Shadow Pictures Double IPA.

DRINK: Todd the Axe Man, their collaboration with Minnesota's Surly, who make a stateside version.

⊰ ROCKY MOUNTAINS ⊱

America's western mountain spine cottoned to craft beer earlier than most. Breweries such as Odell, Avery, and Great Divide created the template for the regional IPAs: sturdily bitter, highly scented with pine and citrus, but enough malt to keep everything in check. Many latest-model IPAs are zeroing in on a dank, marijuana-focused profile—no surprise given the rise of Colorado's legal cannabis dispensaries.

꩜ ODELL IPA

ODELL BREWING CO. | ABV: 7%
FORT COLLINS, COLORADO | AVAILABLE: YEAR-ROUND
ODELLBREWING.COM | GLASS: 🍺 | BITTERNESS: ★★☆☆

The brewery began in 1989 in an old grain elevator, where Doug Odell; wife, Wynne; and sister Corkie devised the Easy Street Wheat Beer and Scottish-inspired 90 Shilling Ale, still the brewery's bestseller. Not far behind stands its orange-gold IPA with its frothy little lingering head. It features plenty of pine needles and grapefruit and a clean, constant bitterness, but it's the perfect balance that will bring you back time and again.

FUN FACT: Odell releases Wolf Picker Pale Ale annually with the same malt bill but different hops, often experimental. The 2016 release tasted like a mango cocktail sipped in a Caribbean sunset.

"During the development stage of our IPA we decided to differentiate ourselves by solely focusing on hop flavor and aroma, as opposed to bitterness. We packed our hopback and added a blend of aromatic American varieties to the fermenter to create a complex hop character with notes of tangerine, grapefruit, peach, pine, and weed. Apparently the judges loved it as much as we did since it won gold at the Great American Beer Festival [2007] and World Beer Cup [2008] immediately following its release."

—Brendan McGivney, COO, Odell Brewing Co.

⸙ MODUS HOPERANDI IPA

SKA BREWING COMPANY | ABV: 6.8%
DURANGO, COLORADO | AVAILABLE: YEAR-ROUND
SKABREWING.COM | GLASS: 🍺 | BITTERNESS: ★★★☆

For the uninitiated, ska is the herky-jerky, horn-slathered, midcentury Jamaican musical genre that combined calypso, jazz, and rhythm and blues. Homebrewing since high school, with a deep appreciation for ska and comic books, buddies Dave Thibodeau and Bill Graham decided in 1995 to unite all three elements in Ska Brewing. Like marijuana, but can't handle the high? You might fall in love with Modus Hoperandi. The IPA has a burnished-orange blast of distilled pine and grapefruit zest kept in check by caramel sweetness and bitterness that they describe poetically as "old man." "We used to smoke a lot of weed, but now we can't handle it, so we just stick with oranges and grapefruits," Thibodeau says. The orange peel–filled Modus Mandarina IPA variant also tastes pretty good.

FUN FACT: In 2003, Ska became America's second craft brewery to can beer, sheathing their Special ESB in aluminum. The brewery now exclusively cans its beer.

BREWERY FOCUS

ODD13 BREWING, LAFAYETTE, COLORADO | ODD13BREWING.COM

Back in 2013, medal-winning homebrewer Ryan Scott and wife, Kristin, conceived the brewery to focus on mixed fermentation and pronounced hops—plenty of aroma and flavor but light on bitterness—along with superhero names and stories. Professor Hops, a *Brettanomyces*-hit India-style saison, "smites his enemies by throwing hop cones that explode into intoxicating clouds of lupulin," and each beer comes with comic-style art worthy of DC or Marvel.

Meanwhile, in Flagstaff, Arizona, Brandon Boldt was preparing to graduate from Northern Arizona University with a master's in geology, but "my fiancée [Lisa] and I thought it'd be fun to take a year off to pursue our hobbies," he says. ("I wanted to explore more styles than what my fake ID would get me," he jokes about his early homebrewing days.) They thought about Oregon, but a Denver friend offered them a couch. Boldt applied to work at Left Hand, New Belgium, and Odd13, about twenty-five miles northwest.

The Scotts hired Boldt to work behind the bar. The big perk? "They let the employees use the pilot brewing system," Boldt says. "It was a great opportunity to get feedback from people who weren't my friends." A few months later, Boldt

applied for the newly vacant position of head brewer. He lacked experience, but he shared with the Scotts his winning love for IPAs.

At Odd13, Boldt oversees a thrilling collection of canned IPAs and sours, often cross-pollinating the styles. "We see ourselves on the really experimental side," he says, noting the Humulus Kalecumber Sour Ale. The portfolio also includes Codename: Superfan, a juicy, hazy take on the Vermont IPA; Hop Troll, an endlessly changing single-malt, single-hop IPA; and Vincent van Couch, a session sour funked up with wild yeast and dry-hopped with Citra and Mosaic. By whirlpool hopping and heavily dry-hopping, Odd13's beers retain more of the ephemeral, volatile hop oils. "We're trying to unlock the potential flavor and aroma of the hops without dragging along the bitterness," Boldt says.

᪥ AVERY IPA

AVERY BREWING CO. | ABV: 6.5%

BOULDER, COLORADO | AVAILABLE: YEAR-ROUND

AVERYBREWING.COM | GLASS: 🍺 | BITTERNESS: ★★☆☆

Adam Avery came to Colorado to rock climb and took a job as an assistant manager at Eastern Mountain Sports, where his boss was a homebrewer. One taste, and the rest was history. If you find yourself down in the dumps, try this boffo mood adjuster: deeply golden, layered with citrus and pine, sticky and resinous, and with a bitterness that any jaded punk-rocker can appreciate. While you're at it, seek out Avery's other IPAs, especially the stronger ones. Look for the royally pungent Maharajah Imperial IPA and its slightly lower-strength sibling, the Raja Double IPA.

🌾 PAKO'S IPA

SNAKE RIVER BREWING | ABV: 6.8%

JACKSON, WYOMING | AVAILABLE: YEAR-ROUND

SNAKERIVERBREWING.COM | GLASS: 🍺 | BITTERNESS: ★★☆☆

Beginning in 1994 as a brewpub, Snake River is Wyoming's oldest brewery. Brewmaster Chris Erickson has been steering the ship since 1996 and created this gold-medal grabber (Great American Beer Festival 2011). Named for the brewpub's mascot, which had a blue and black eye—think Eye-P-A—Pako's is ruggedly golden and freighted with Simcoe and Columbus hops. No tropical fruit here, just pine resin and citrus zest in all their goosed-up, pungent glory.

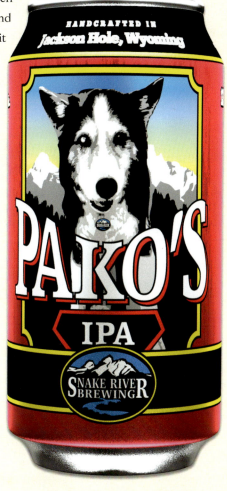

IPA ITINERARY
⚑ COLORADO ⚑

Air holds less moisture at higher altitudes, so hydrate! For the latest info about Colorado's breweries, visit coloradobeer.org.

DAY 1: DENVER

Commence at **COMRADE BREWING** Ⓐ (7667 E. Iliff Ave., comradebrewing .com) with El Nuggarillo IPA, tropical Hop Chops Double IPA, and cult star Superpower (page 000). Refill at **RENEGADE** Ⓑ (925 W. 9th Ave., renegadebrewing .com) with their best-selling Redacted Rye IPA, a citrus-peppery prelude to the Endpoint Triple IPA, single-hopped with Summit. Visit the huge tasting room at

EPIC BREWING **C** (3001 Walnut St., epicbrewing.com) and savor their imperial IPA. River North, Denver's hottest brewing neighborhood, also includes wild-focused **CROOKED STAVE** **D** (3350 Brighton Blvd., crookedstave.com) and **RATIO BEERWORKS** **E** (2920 Larimer St., ratiobeerworks.com), which serves the West Coast–style Antidote IPA. Venture north to **BLACK SHIRT BREWING** **F** (3719 Walnut St., blackshirtbrewingco.com) for Red Evelyn, an imperial red rye IPA, or the double IPA dolled up with blood oranges, then call it a day at **STATION 26** **G** (7045 E 38th Ave., station26brewing.co) with any of the single-hop IPAs or the Juicy Banger IPA.

DAY 2: BOULDER

Detour to Golden, birthplace of Coors and **CANNONBALL CREEK** **H** (393 Washington Ave., cannonballcreekbrewing.com), which serves Featherweight Pale Ale, one of America's finest, and Mindbender IPA, booming with grapefruit. Go north to **FATE BREWING COMPANY** **I** (1600 38th St., fatebrewingcompany .com) for IPAs infused with cold-brew coffee and seasoned with salt or chile peppers. Shoot over to **SANITAS** **J** (3550 Frontier Ave., sanitasbrewing.com) to play bocce while sipping their IPA range. Then visit **UPSLOPE** **K** (1898 S. Flatiron Ct., upslopebrewing.com) for their experimental and imperial IPAs, and crown day two at **AVERY** **L** (4910 Nautilus Ct., averybrewing.com) for taproom-only releases (in the downstairs bar), such as Winter's Day IPA, seasoned with rosemary and lemon zest, and dark sour ales aged in tequila barrels.

DAY 3: FORT COLLINS

At Longmont's **OSKAR BLUES HOME MADE LIQUIDS AND SOLIDS** **M** (1555 S. Hover Rd., oskarbluesfooderies.com), grease your system while drinking the Pinner Session IPA chased with Deviant Dale's Double IPA. Go north to **LEFT HAND** **N** (1265 Boston Ave., lefthandbrewing.com), and kick back with the Introvert Session IPA and the English-inspired 400 Pound Monkey IPA. In Fort Collins, first up is **FUNKWERKS** **O** (1900 E. Lincoln Ave., funkwerks.com). Try the Nelson Sauvin and imperial Tropic King, rocked with Rakau. Onward to **ODELL BREWING** **P** (800 E Lincoln Ave., odellbrewing.com) for the brisk Loose Leaf Session IPA and tropical Myrcenary Double IPA. End at **NEW BELGIUM** **Q** (500 Linden St., newbelgium.com) for a top-notch tour and the Slow Ride Session IPA.

⬡ INCREDIBLE PEDAL IPA

DENVER BEER CO. | ABV: 7%

DENVER, COLORADO | AVAILABLE: YEAR-ROUND

DENVERBEERCO.COM | GLASS: 🍺 | BITTERNESS: ★★☆☆

In 2011, an old car garage became one of the Mile High City's finest breweries. DBC specializes in beers that sound strange—Graham Cracker Porter, Pueblo Chili Beer, Kaffir Lime Wheat—but taste great. Incredible Pedal
cruises a slightly more orthodox road, though. Crack the can, and breathe
deep to fill your head with mango, papaya, and citrus zest. Incredible isn't
as dry as a SoCal IPA. It has a modest amount of caramel malt and a finish
summed up in a single word: grapefruit.

🌾 SUPERPOWER IPA

COMRADE BREWING | ABV: 7%

DENVER, COLORADO | AVAILABLE: YEAR-ROUND

COMRADEBREWING.COM | GLASS: 🍺 BITTERNESS: ★★☆☆

Marks Lanham brewed at Idaho's Grand Teton, Oregon's Boneyard, and Barley Brown's Beer, cooking up Pallet Jack IPA (page 127), regularly named one of America's best. At Comrade, hotly desired hops, such as Citra, Amarillo, and Simcoe, are brothers in arms. The trio create the honeyed-orange Superpower, which pops with plenty of juicy grapefruit, pine, and guava and a deep, abiding dankness. The malt offers a structural support of light sweetness, like sugar-dusted toast. Simply put: This is one of Colorado's best new-breed IPAs.

When in Denver, sip Superpower at Falling Rock, one of America's best beer joints bar none.

🌾 TITAN IPA

GREAT DIVIDE BREWING COMPANY | ABV: 7.1%

DENVER, COLORADO | AVAILABLE: YEAR-ROUND

GREATDIVIDE.COM | GLASS: 🍺 | BITTERNESS: ★★★☆

Yeti is Great Divide's top-billed star, a delicious imperial stout designed to stomp your senses, but dig into their portfolio to find a deep and deft appreciation for hops. The palate-piquing Lasso Session IPA will rope you in; the potent Hercules Double IPA will clobber your taste buds; and Titan recalls an earlier era of calibrated aggression: Its caramel-focused rush of piney bitterness and grapefruit zest, resinous and malty, offers a reminder that sometimes your senses deserve a good, solid rattling.

FUN FACT: First brewed in 2003, Great Divide's Fresh Hop Ale predated most. The brewery used express shipping to source the Pacific Northwest hops that go into the drink-now fall specialty.

🌾 ESCAPE TO COLORADO

EPIC BREWING | ABV: 6.2%

DENVER, COLORADO; SALT LAKE CITY, UTAH | AVAILABLE: YEAR-ROUND

EPICBREWING.COM | GLASS: 🍺 | BITTERNESS: ★★☆☆

For a Utah brewery focusing on higher-test offerings, Colorado has more lenient alcohol laws, so for its second facility Epic located here, commemorating the expansion with this semi-hazy gold IPA, powered by Apollo and Mosaic, that provides a whiff of mango, passion fruit, and grapefruit aromatics that also glide across the tongue, bright and painless, working in concert with bread and low-bore bitterness. Also try Epic's Brainless series of Belgian-inspired beers, including a commendably fruity IPA.

⊨ SOUTHWEST ⊨

Scorching daytime heat demands an increased dryness that sacrifices sweetness but celebrates pine and citrus, which you'll find in Southwestern IPAs from Arizona Wilderness and La Cumbre. Cooler nights favor bitter beers with a chunk of old-school malt sweetness, which COOP Ale Works and Deep Ellum deliver.

⬇ ELEVATED IPA

LA CUMBRE BREWING COMPANY | ABV: 7.2%
ALBUQUERQUE, NEW MEXICO | AVAILABLE: YEAR-ROUND
LACUMBREBREWING.COM | GLASS: 🍺 | BITTERNESS: ★★★☆

In 2010, Jeff Erway and his wife founded La Cumbre and within eighteen months had grabbed gold at 2011's Great American Beer Festival for this wheat-touched, grapefruit-heightened IPA. Made with a blend of seven hops, the aroma delivers a dizzying swirl that, depending on the wind, might smell floral or herbal, with whiffs of pine, peaches, or weed. "Today's IPAs are all about hitting a balance between the enormous juicy hop aromatics that entice the drinker and the required bracing bitterness expected from a beer that smells so fragrant," he says. "Malt, while it does play a role, need not interfere much, and yeast is simply there to provide the requisite alcohol." By pitching 40 percent of the recommended yeast, this desert-dry IPA also ferments faster and healthier. "What matters to our fans is that the beer has a rich, dank bouquet. It should represent not just an alcoholic beverage at the end of their day but a compelling experience every time they drink our beers."

⬩ REFUGE IPA

ARIZONA WILDERNESS BREWING CO. | ABV: 7.2%
GILBERT, ARIZONA | AVAILABLE: YEAR-ROUND
AZWBEER.COM | GLASS: 🍺 | BITTERNESS: ★★☆☆

Jonathan Buford ran a window-cleaning business but unearthed the inspiration to found Arizona Wilderness after watching *Brew Masters*, Dogfish Head–founder Sam Calagione's TV show. No need to go off the grid to find this brewery, which sits in a strip mall southeast of Phoenix. "Wilderness" refers to both the notion that beer, like the wild, must be protected and to the region's recipe-inspiring vistas and foraged ingredients. Taste the Grand Canyon State in the drily refreshing Table Top Saison, containing Sonoran white wheat. The Futures Saison features wild prickly pear cactus, and spruce tips spice the Pine Mountain Sour Pale. Forever on tap is Refuge, a West Coast–leaning IPA chockablock with hops in a fragrant exultation of grapefruit and pine with a subtle substructure of biscuits and caramel.

⛁ DEEP ELLUM IPA

DEEP ELLUM BREWING COMPANY I ABV: 7%

DALLAS, TEXAS I AVAILABLE: YEAR-ROUND

DEEPELLUMBREWING.COM I GLASS: 🍺 I BITTERNESS: ★★☆☆

In its agenda-setting "beerfesto," this brewery made a series of strong pledges that include ignoring gimmicks, letting the brews speak loudest, and crucially, "never to serve a single glass of bad beer." Following those tenets, they've created solidly built, honest sippers, such as the floral Dallas Blonde, corn-laced Neato Bandito Lager, and dark and fruity Four Swords Belgian-style Quadruple. Dreamcrusher is a bitter yet malt-sweet double IPA, and the flag-ship IPA takes inspiration from the Pacific Northwest, particularly Amarillo, Citra, and Chinook hops. Heaped alongside honey and Vienna malts and a smidgen of white wheat, the auburn-orange IPA tastes judiciously saccha-rine, generously floral, and crowded with flavors of peaches, pine trees, and grapefruit. Buy it by the can.

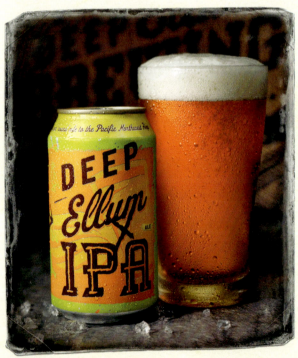

🌾 YELLOW ROSE

THE LONE PINT BREWERY | ABV: 6.6%
MAGNOLIA, TEXAS | AVAILABLE: YEAR-ROUND
LONEPINT.COM | GLASS: 🍺 | BITTERNESS: ★☆☆☆

Siblings Trevor Brown and Heather Niederhofer spent six years brewing in a garage on a 20-gallon system before turning an auto-body shop in Magnolia—northeast of Houston, population: almost 1,400—into Lone Pint. They traffic in unfiltered, unpasteurized ales made with whole-cone hops, including the pungent Jabberwocky Double IPA and the Zythophile series of single-hop IPAs. Their biggest smash is Yellow Rose, a SMASH IPA—single malt and single hop, that is—powered by pilsner malt and Mosaic hops. The combo produces a smooth and hazy-gold sipping experience, more juicy than bitter and mobbed with blueberries and grapefruit in bouquet and taste.

FUN FACT: *Zythophile* means beer lover.

BREWERY FOCUS

SANTAN BREWING, CHANDLER, ARIZONA | SANTANBREWING.COM

For almost eight years, Anthony Canecchia toiled at Four Peaks in Tempe, Arizona, turning out Scotch ales and English-inspired beers that toed the traditional line. "I got really tired of making big, sweet, sticky English ales," he says. Why not brew something new, using the latest generation of hops, such as Amarillo? "I kept imploring my former boss," he says. The answer: No.

Canecchia left Four Peaks in 2007 to found SanTan. First order of business was deploying newly developed hops, notably New Zealand's Nelson Sauvin. "It absolutely blew me away," he recalls of the white-wine-and-gooseberry varietal. ("I look forward to the first time I'll ever have a gooseberry," he says.) He sourced them direct from New Zealand Hop Limited, cost be damned. "That's how enthralled I was with that hop," says Canecchia, who uses that variety and Australia's Galaxy in both his peachy and zesty HopShock and island-succulent MoonJuice IPAs. "You see the look on people's faces the first time they drink it. They think they're drinking a fruit beer," he says, of MoonJuice, part of his dry, refreshing, effervescent portfolio of southwestern ales.

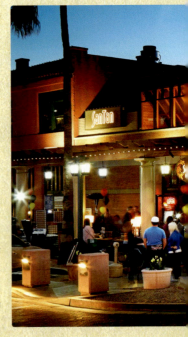

"I wanted to make beers for the Arizona climate," Canecchia explains, and his IPAs are acclimatizing southwestern drinkers to the notion that hoppy beers need not taste like a knockout punch. "Any idiot can dump a bunch of hops at the front end of the boil and make something very bitter," he says. "We want to create these amazing tropical flavors so beers are more hop-forward without being bitter. People are looking for beer that's not one-dimensional. They're not looking for that big, southpaw left hook in the jaw."

SanTan's other hits are as memorable as they are food-friendly. Try the Mr. Pineapple Wheat Ale with tacos al pastor, the SunSpot Gold with pizza, and the Sex Panther Double Chocolate Porter with smoked meats or dessert.

A PALE MOSAIC

HOPS & GRAIN | ABV: 5.93%

AUSTIN, TEXAS | AVAILABLE: YEAR-ROUND

HOPSANDGRAIN.COM | GLASS: 🍺 | BITTERNESS: ★☆☆☆

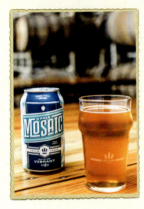

This unfiltered IPA is a rare creature: a clean-drinking, gluggable IPA that offers a paragon for the category's structure. The downright dainty ABV, gelato smoothness, and unobtrusive body serve as a platform for the main event, showcasing the berry-like, piney, and grapefruit grandeur of Mosaic hops. Also check out the Greenhouse IPA, a ceaseless exploration of new hop varieties.

FUN FACT: The sustainability-focused Hop & Grain transforms its spent grain into dog treats called Brew Biscuits.

MARBLE IPA

MARBLE BREWERY | ABV: 6.8%

ALBUQUERQUE, NEW MEXICO | AVAILABLE: YEAR-ROUND

MARBLEBREWERY.COM | GLASS: 🍺 | BITTERNESS: ★★★☆

Since debuting in an industrial warehouse in 2008, Marble has become a medal magnet. Brewer Ted Rice has a natural facility with traditional styles, such as the unfiltered Pilsner and Belgian-inspired Double White alongside hop-wallopers like the piney imperial red, funky Brett IPA, and juicy double IPA. The intensely golden, base-strength IPA—a superb match with spicy southwestern cuisine—teems with six hops, including Citra, Simcoe, and Mosaic, which provide loads of lemon peel cut with apricots and mangos. Resin and caramel-sweet malt play supporting roles.

FUN FACT: Marble released two IPAs to commemorate the final season of *Breaking Bad*, filmed in Albuquerque: Heisenberg's Dark and Walt's White Lie.

HOP KNOT IPA

FOUR PEAKS BREWING COMPANY | ABV: 6.7%
TEMPE, ARIZONA | AVAILABLE: YEAR-ROUND
FOURPEAKS.COM | GLASS: 🍺 | BITTERNESS: ★★☆☆

Conceived in 1996 in a former creamery, Four Peaks has risen to the top of Arizona's brewing ranks with its kölsch-inspired Sunbru and Kilt Lifter, a faintly smoky Scottish-style ale. Named after a quartet of elevations in the nearby Mazatzal Mountains, Four Peaks ups the IPA game with throwbacks like Raj, a fruity and earthy English IPA. A hop quintet (Simcoe, Liberty, Cascade, Glacier, and Magnum added at different stages) ties together the more current Hop Knot, a flaxen IPA that tastes like a pine tree snuggling up to an orange grove under a bittersweet blanket.

FUN FACT: AB InBev purchased Four Peaks in 2015.

❦ F5 IPA

COOP ALE WORKS | ABV: 6.8%

OKLAHOMA CITY, OKLAHOMA | AVAILABLE: YEAR-ROUND

COOPALEWORKS.COM | GLASS: 🍺 | BITTERNESS: ★★★☆

Prior to becoming COOP's head brewer, Blake Jarolim taught middle school and homebrewed as a hobby. Falconer's Flight, a carefully calibrated hops blend named for brewing pioneer Glen Hay Falconer, includes Simcoe, Sorachi Ace, and Citra as well as several secret hops. That mixture partners with Columbus hops in F5—the strongest tornado classification—acknowledging that COOP sits in Tornado Alley. The orange-gold IPA spins orange, pineapple, and coniferous trees, while caramel sweetness and pithy bitterness keep it rooted. Also try their buzzy Alpha Hive, a double IPA dosed with orange blossom honey.

BREWERY SPOTLIGHT

CERVEZA CUCAPÀ | MEXICALI, BAJA CALIFORNIA 🇲🇽

Named for a tribe native to the area, this groundbreaking brewery has been showing drinkers since 2002 that a beer can have bitterness, flavor, and a sense of humor. For example: their imperial stout is named La Migra, short for immigration police. They also make barley wines aged in tequila barrels alongside accessible blonde ales and the Chupacabras Pale Ale.

DRINK: Runaway IPA, a fine piney, herbal complement to spicy Mexican fare.

⊯ WEST COAST ⊱

In 1871, Gottlieb Brekle, a German brewer, bought a San Francisco billiards saloon on Pacific Avenue and turned it into what became the Anchor Brewing Company. Fritz Maytag, the washer-dryer heir, saved Anchor from closure in 1965 and, in the process of reversing the brewery's fortunes, catalyzed the craft beer movement. A decade after that, Anchor's Liberty Ale became the first modern IPA brewed after Prohibition and the first beer to use a single hop exclusively (Cascade, debuted in 1972 by Oregon State University). For many, the crisp California IPA represents the new, lean-drinking American archetype, thanks to the efforts of AleSmith, Green Flash, Stone, and others. Often golden, West Coast IPAs feature an unobtrusive malt structure that supports copious amounts of pine and grapefruit with the occasional mango and papaya thrown in for flavorful fun.

🌾 SCULPIN

BALLAST POINT BREWING COMPANY | ABV: 7%
SAN DIEGO, CALIFORNIA | AVAILABLE: YEAR-ROUND
BALLASTPOINT.COM | GLASS: | BITTERNESS: ★★☆☆

Born in a back room of Home Brew Mart in 1996, Ballast Point makes a lot of great IPAs: the Big Eye, session-strength Even Keel, and the Fathom IPL. Choosing just one proved difficult, but Sculpin, named for a tasty fish with venomous fins, accounts for the lion's share of sales. The first taste stings a little, but a rush of stone fruit and a tropical fruit buffet absolve any pain. Given the ABV, it's criminally easy to crush bottle after bottle, can after can. Sculpin evolved from a homebrew recipe and has spawned a number of offshoots, including Habanero, Pineapple, and Grapefruit.

FUN FACT: Ballast Point also operates a prolific distillery division, doing right by gin, rum, vodka, and whiskey. Better still, they can premixed cocktails, including the Fugu Bloody Mary and Old Grove Gin and Tonic. Corona importer Constellation Brands bought Ballast Point in 2015 for $1 billion.

A rising IPA star on Northern California's brewing scene is Fieldwork. Cofounder Alex Tweet previously brewed at Modern Times and Ballast Point.

🌾 ALESMITH IPA

ALESMITH BREWING COMPANY | ABV: 7.25%
SAN DIEGO, CALIFORNIA | AVAILABLE: YEAR-ROUND
ALESMITH.COM | GLASS: 🍺 | BITTERNESS: ★★☆☆

Inaugurated in 1995, AleSmith recently embarked on an ambitious expansion plan, aiming to spread the brewery's beers both nationally and globally—a smart move, given that Rate Beer decreed it the world's best brewery for 2014. AleSmith's expertise spans a world of styles, nailing ESBs, nut browns, barley wines, and Belgian-style strong ales, such as the fruity and spicy Horny Devil. They hammer out good IPAs as well, including the summer and winter Double and Double Red IPAs and their namesake IPA, which is everything you want in a San Diego IPA: orange-gold, scented with grapefruit and pine, dry, and crisply carbonated. The bitterness is resinous and moderate but insistent.

FUN FACT: Danish gypsy brewer Mikkeller now occupies AleSmith's old brewery.

" 'Balance' isn't a bad word when describing IPAs, so we pay a lot of the attention to the malt bill. We use adequate malt to support an imaginary thing we refer to as the 'wall of hops.' Certain specialty malts create a perfect bridge to the hops and help create flavors of stone fruit, citrus, and tropical fruits. Attention to malt is every bit as important as attention to the hops."

—Peter Zien, owner and brewmaster, AleSmith Brewing

IPA ITINERARY
⇒ SAN DIEGO ⇐

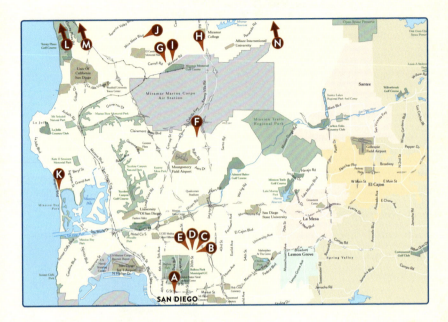

For the latest info on San Diego's breweries and
brewpubs, visit sandiegobrewersguild.org.

DAY 1: NORTH PARK

Start in the East Village's **MONKEY PAW PUB AND BREWERY** Ⓐ (805 16th St.,
monkeypawbrewing.com) with the deceptively strong Bonobos IPA and the San
Diego–defining Howler and Cornelius double IPAs. Wind northeast to
MODERN TIMES FLAVORDOME Ⓑ (3000 Upas St., moderntimesbeer.com) for
the fruity City of the Sun IPA and dank, amber Blazing World. Hit **MIKE HESS
BREWING** Ⓒ (3812 Grim Ave., mikehessbrewing.com) for the rye-spicy Habitus
Double IPA before visiting **RIP CURRENT BREWING & SUBLIME ALE HOUSE** Ⓓ
(4101 30th St., ripcurrentbrewing.com) for the standard and double Lupulin

Lust IPAs. A few blocks north awaits **BELCHING BEAVER** Ⓔ (4223 30th St., belchinbeaver.com) and its medal-winning Rabid Beaver Rye IPA, Dammed! Double IPA, and Pound Town, a triple that took top honors at 2014's Alpha King Challenge. Still thirsty? Get thee to **SOCIETE BREWING** Ⓕ (8262 Clairemont Mesa Blvd., societebrewing.com) for the 2015 GABF gold-winning Coachman Session IPA.

DAY 2: GO NORTH

Venture to the Miramar branch of **BALLAST POINT** Ⓖ (9045 Carroll Way, ballastpoint.com) for one of the Sculpin IPA variants and R&D IPAs made with oats and special cask ales. **WHITE LABS** Ⓗ (9495 Candida St., whitelabs.com), a yeast supplier, operates a nerd-worthy, must-visit tasting room. Then proceed to the new **ALESMITH** Ⓘ brewery (9990 AleSmith Ct., alesmith.com) for its essential IPA, hop-centric collaborations with Mikkeller, and San Diego Pale Ale .394, named for local baseball legend Tony Gwynn. Alight to **GREEN FLASH BREWING** Ⓙ (6550 Mira Mesa Blvd., greenflashbrew.com) for the garden and tasting room, where you can load up on single, double, or triple IPAs.

DAY 3: HOP UP THE PACIFIC

Hug the coast for Pacific Beach's **AMPLIFIED ALE WORKS** Ⓚ (4150 Mission Blvd., amplifiedales.com) and their tropical, orangey Electrocution IPA. Go north to Solana Beach, home to **PIZZA PORT** Ⓛ (135 N. Hwy 101, pizzaport.com) and its collection of hop-forward ales, including Simcoe City and Swami's, one of the early examples of the San Diego IPA. Continue north to Oceanside's **BAGBY BEER COMPANY** Ⓜ (601 S. Coast Hwy., bagbybeer.com) for the fruity, cleanly balanced Dork Squad or the Weissenhopper, a hoppy German-style wheat beer. Head inland to Escondido for **STONE BREWING** Ⓝ (1999 Citracado Pkwy., stonebrewing.com). Their Stone's World Bistro & Gardens serves a range of beer-infused food paired with IPAs, such as the Cali-Belgique and gluten-free Delicious. They also serve pilot and vintage beers for those seeking something unusual.

"San Diego is synonymous with awesome IPAs," says Mike Sardina, past president of the San Diego Brewers Guild. "It's almost always the perfect day for a beer."

⬇ DUET

ALPINE BEER COMPANY | ABV: 7%

ALPINE, CALIFORNIA | AVAILABLE: ROTATING

ALPINEBEERCO.COM | GLASS: 🍺 | BITTERNESS: ★★☆☆

Firefighter and homebrewer Pat McIlhenney had a hankering to go pro, so in 1999 he tapped AleSmith to make contract-brews, including Pure Hoppiness, a double IPA "so mega-hopped it will take you to hop heaven" (probably an understatement). In 2002, he opened Alpine, the portfolio ablaze with bitterness and in time featuring the rye-spiked Nelson and Exponential Hoppiness Imperial IPA. For a primer on their liquid artwork, try the floral and clean Duet, a harmonious convergence of Amarillo and Simcoe hops, citrusy, light, and nimble.

FUN FACT: Green Flash acquired Alpine in 2014, so expect to see wider and deeper production and distribution.

🌾 THE PUPIL

SOCIETE BREWING COMPANY | ABV: 7.5%

SAN DIEGO, CALIFORNIA | AVAILABLE: YEAR-ROUND

SOCIETEBREWING.COM | GLASS: 🍺 | BITTERNESS: ★★☆☆

Travis Smith and Doug Constantiner punched the clock at California's most cultish IPA breweries, including Russian River, Pizza Port, and Bruery, prior to starting Societe, which expectedly specializes in pale ales, dark ales, Belgian-style saisons, and IPAs of every permutation, all of them high class. Their Apprentice IPA wholeheartedly embraces piney bitterness, but it's the straw-gold, medium-bodied Pupil that will quicken your pulse. The pure, undiluted tropical fruit—mangos mixed with pineapples and maybe some guava—masterfully cloaks the alcohol with bitterness barely there and dryness verging on a fire warning. The Coachman session IPA is also a total crusher.

⚜ AMALGAMATOR

BEACHWOOD BBQ & BREWING | ABV: 7.1%

LONG BEACH, CALIFORNIA | AVAILABLE: YEAR-ROUND

BEACHWOODBBQ.COM | GLASS: 🍺 | BITTERNESS: ★★★☆

Beachwood's ingenious draft system, dubbed the Flux Capacitor (pictured below), enables bartenders to calibrate an individual serving's temperature and pressure, ensuring proper pours of Udder Love Milk Stout, Full Malted Jacket Scotch Ale, and Foam Top Cream Ale. Engineer-turned-brewer Julian Shrago has also mastered the dry, aroma-rocked West Coast IPA with the juicy-sticky Resinator, piney and citrusy Melrose, and the Amalgamator. It has a light two-row malt foundation laden with Amarillo, Warrior, Columbus, and Mosaic, the last of which drives the dry-hopping. The cracker-dry result fuses papayas and passion fruit, oranges and grapefruit, and resin from a freshly used one-hitter.

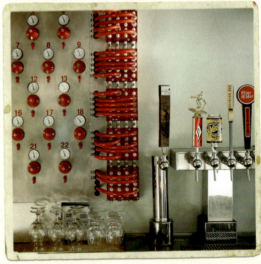

🌾 JUST OUTSTANDING

KERN RIVER BREWING COMPANY | ABV: 6.8%

KERNVILLE, CALIFORNIA | AVAILABLE: YEAR-ROUND

KERNRIVERBREWING.COM | GLASS: 🍺 | BITTERNESS: ★★★☆

In 2006, firefighting homebrewer Kyle Smith teamed with Olympic kayaker-spouses Eric and Rebecca Giddens to create Kern River, perched on the southern edge of the Sierra Nevada. Citra, their much-lauded double IPA, is nearly impossible to find. Instead, go for the attainable pleasure of Just Outstanding. The tawny-orange California IPA has solid malt-sweet scaffolding for a delightfully weedy flower-shop bouquet that drives into citrus-rind bitterness. One taste, and the name makes perfect sense.

BREWERY FOCUS

CELLARMAKER BREWING, SAN FRANCISCO, CALIFORNIA | CELLARMAKERBREWING.COM

At San Francisco's City Beer Store, one of the Bay Area's best, Connor Casey kept a close eye on the refrigerator. "I watched people pillage the fridges for IPAs all day long. I realized the IPA is not dead, but people are dissatisfied with the IPAs they can get. The best ones sell out every day." That was his epiphany: "Let's make something different. Let's change the game and drive the flavors of real fruits from hops and serve it hyper, hyper fresh."

And insanely fresh they are at Cellarmaker, a 10-barrel operation founded by Casey and head brewer Tim Sciascia, whom he met at Marin Brewing. They specialize in new, rarely repeated pales ales and IPAs. "We've tried to create a brand where people trust us as a company, not for our beers," says Casey. Dankster, Tiny Dankster, Highway to the Danker Zone, and New Beer Smell are lightly bitter, juicy, and dripping with new-breed and experimental varietals such as Citra, Equinox, and South Africa's Southern Passion, drought-dry and

radiant as noon in the Mojave. "On the beer list we'll put 'notes of papaya and mango,' and people will ignore that and say, 'How much papaya and mango did you put in this?' That's the biggest compliment we can have."

Freshness is paramount. "I don't drink hoppy beer past day ten or fifteen," Casey says. "You taste the hops more than ever when it's hoppy beer direct out of a brite tank and two days old." To ensure that freshness, Cellarmaker's invoices require that bars keep the beer cold and serve it within seven days. "Hoppy beer is like milk," says Casey. "People should drink it right away. If you taste an IPA that's only a day old, you're hooked."

Cellarmaker revels in expanding horizons as well. "I love getting the customer who is like, 'I don't like IPA,' " Casey says. "I give them an IPA that's like 45 IBUs, and they're like, 'Oh my God, this is so cool.' " They also make saisons and blondes, lightly smoky porters and pilsners, creating new pathways between retooled styles and ardent fans.

🌾 ISLANDER IPA

CORONADO BREWING COMPANY | ABV: 7%

CORONADO, CALIFORNIA | AVAILABLE: YEAR-ROUND

CORONADOBREWING.COM | GLASS: 🍺 | BITTERNESS: ★★☆☆

Coronado lies on a peninsula connected to San Diego by a slender isthmus, and their Islander is a perfect poster child for a Southern California IPA. It's rocket-boosted with citrusy Centennial, pine-drenched Chinook, and spicy-earthy Columbus hops, a triumvirate that drives a lightly hazy, gold-plated road sticky and studded with fresh biscuits—and no blackballing the malt here. Keep an eye out for other Coronado releases, specifically the staunchly bitter, imperial-strength Idiot and Stingray, swimming with tropical verve.

SAN FRANCISCO IPA

ALMANAC BEER CO. | ABV: 6.5%
SAN FRANCISCO, CALIFORNIA | AVAILABLE: YEAR-ROUND
ALMANACBEER.COM | GLASS: 🍺 | BITTERNESS: ★★☆☆

The farm-to-barrel philosophy steers Almanac, which digs into its local watershed to make beers like Golden Gate Gose, seasoned with San Francisco Bay salt, and the Farmer's Reserve series of sour, barrel-aged beers infused with local fruit. San Francisco IPA is part of Almanac's Fresh Beer Series, focusing on huge flavor and aromas plus expressive yeast, canned quickly and sold even faster. That means a clean, oat-enhanced IPA dankly draped with West Coast hops, including El Dorado, Citra, and Mosaic, and Germany's wine-like Hallertau Blanc cultivar. It's a tropical tapestry, ideally stitched to one hand while the other palms a burrito.

FUN FACT: Previously a graphic designer, cofounder Damian Fagan designs all of Almanac's labels.

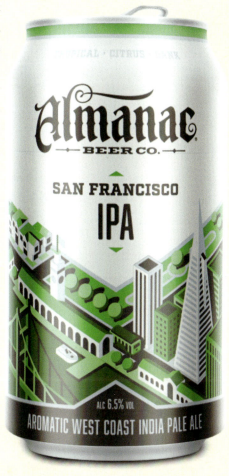

BREWERY SPOTLIGHT

HONG KONG BEER CO. | HONG KONG, CHINA

Founded in 1995 as South China Brewing Company, Hong Kong underwent a relaunch, installing Pyramid Brewery's Simon Tesch as brewmaster and rolling out beers to suit both sides of the Pacific, among them: Sevens Stout; White Pearl Witbier spiced with rosebuds, honey, and Mandarin orange peel; and the dry-hopped Dragon's Back Pale Ale.

DRINK: Big Wave Bay, a West Coast–inspired IPA brimming with Australian and American hops.

MOOR BEER CO. | BRISTOL, ENGLAND

Founded on a dairy farm in 1996, Moor had a rocky adolescence before Justin and Maryann Hawke, former U.S. Army officers, bought the brewery and retooled it to focus on unfiltered, naturally hazy ales high on hops and flavor. Hemispherically opposed hops separate the low-strength Nor'hop and So'hop pales, while Illusion takes the black IPA to session country.

DRINK: Hoppiness, a golden California-style IPA that tastes piney, grassy, and fruity with balancing malt sweetness.

꞊ PACIFIC NORTHWEST ꞊

Founded in 1982 in an old opera house, Bert Grant's Yakima Brewing and Malting Co. dragged the India pale ale from the history bin. First brewed in 1983, Grant's generously aromatic, highly hopped ale sat around 60 IBUs, its vibrant label featuring the Taj Mahal and the word *IPA*—the first modern American brewery to use the word there. He laid the groundwork for the region's IPAs, later refined by Portland's BridgePort, which adjusted local palates with 1996's then-groundbreaking IPA packed with five hop varieties, including Cascade and Chinook. Today, cool temperatures, lots of rain, and proximity to the nation's finest hop fields create the recipe for the Pacific Northwest IPA, grounded with darker malts, such as crystal and Munich, and heightened with citrus and plenty of pine resin. These IPAs form the archetype of modern craft brewing.

♦ BREAKSIDE IPA

BREAKSIDE BREWERY | ABV: 6.4%
PORTLAND, OREGON | AVAILABLE: YEAR-ROUND
BREAKSIDE.COM | GLASS: 🍺 | BITTERNESS: ★★☆☆

Here Ben Edmunds, one of America's best brewers, applies his creative, scientifically rigorous mind to a dizzying range of brews, including a dry-hopped sour ale that's tart and tropical, a salted caramel dessert stout, and even cocktail-inspired beers. (Think Sazerac and Whiskey Ginger.) More impressively, he nails classics like the pilsner and IPA. The clear amber Breakside sets the paradigm for the Pacific Northwest IPA. It's a lightly caramel-sweet clean-drinker that tastes like a pine forest crowned with a bowl of tropical fruit. Dig the darker side? Go for the golden, grapefruity Wanderlust IPA.

"In thinking about how the Northwest IPA might differ from the IPAs being brewed in other regions, I'd identify two unique characteristics. First are the relationships with hop farmers. Our proximity to the main hop-growing regions allows almost all of our hop-focused breweries to travel to Yakima for hop selection. There's a level of quality and focus in hoppy beers that comes from selecting your hop lots, and it's a geographical advantage. Second, and this is more in the flavor realm, I think that Northwest IPAs are defined by a refined and balanced bitterness. In the best examples from our region, you can taste how bitterness can be a pleasant and key structural part of a hoppy beer; a complement to the aromas and flavors of hops and malt."

🌾 TOPCUTTER IPA

BALE BREAKER BREWING COMPANY | ABV: 6.8%
YAKIMA, WASHINGTON | AVAILABLE: YEAR-ROUND
BALEBREAKER.COM | GLASS: 🍺 | BITTERNESS: ★★☆☆

In 1932, Meghan Quinn and Kevin Smith's great-grandparents founded B. T. Loftus Ranches, now run by their older brother. Smith, Quinn, and her husband, Kevin, converted three acres of Field 41 into Bale Breaker. Sister handles marketing, and brother brews hop-forward beers, such as the grassy, citrusy Field 41 Pale Ale and America's freshest wet-hop beers—field to kettle in five minutes! Named for the machine that trims hop bines from trellises, the sturdily built, hazy orange Topcutter swirls with aromas of grapefruit and caramel that pine sap joins on the palate.

NOT SO FUN FACT: A 2006 fire destroyed a major Yakima hops warehouse. The next year, drought, disease, and floods decimated crops across America and Europe. A hop shortage soon swept the world.

HOPWORKS IPA

HOPWORKS URBAN BREWERY | ABV: 6.6%
PORTLAND, OREGON | AVAILABLE: YEAR-ROUND
HOPWORKSBEER.COM | GLASS: 🍺 | BITTERNESS: ★★☆☆

Brewing recently endured a craze for organic ingredients, in which provenance mattered more than the recipe. Breweries that pulled off both were rarer than a one-legged unicyclist. Christian Ettinger's brewery is one of them, championing both cycling and crackerjack organic ingredients that power lagers, coffee stouts, and white IPAs containing wheat grown on the family farm. (The grain also goes into Nonstop Hef Hop, a low-alcohol revitalizer, like a beer drinker's Gatorade.) The Hopworks IPA, a Pacific Northwest classic, offers a resinous riot of pine and citrus laced with just enough toasty sweetness to keep everything in equilibrium. In other words: It's a classic ride.

FUN FACT: What's better than beer or biking? A festival celebrating both! Hopworks hosts the annual Handmade Bike & Beer Festival, which welcomes bands, bike builders, and brewers such as Base Camp, the Commons, and pFriem Family.

🌾 RPM IPA

BONEYARD BEER | ABV: 6.5%
BEND, OREGON | AVAILABLE: YEAR-ROUND
BONEYARDBEER.COM | GLASS: 🍺 | BITTERNESS: ★★☆☆

Like sending a hunter into the wild to bag a duck or a buck, recommending a draft-only beer is hit-or-miss—but in this case it's worth it. Deschutes alum Tony Lawrence ran a brewery construction and consulting business that acquired equipment from brewery boneyards, storage places for unwanted equipment. By 2010, he had accrued enough of the necessary pieces to assemble Boneyard Beer. His calling card quickly became hop-hammered formulations, including the Hop Venom Double and Notorious Triple IPAs. Boneyard's bread and butter is RPM, a shimmering russet-gold vision of citrus and pineapple. Give it a spin the next time you're in Oregon or Washington.

FUN FACT: Boneyard supplies the wort to make Dawg Grog, a nutritious beverage for man's best friend. It doesn't contain hops, though, which are toxic to certain breeds of pooches.

BREWERY FOCUS

BARLEY BROWN'S, BAKER CITY, OREGON | BARLEYBROWNSBEER.COM

You don't arrive in Baker City by accident. "We're 304 miles from Portland and not really on the way to anything," Tyler Brown says of his high-desert hometown and an erstwhile Oregon Trail hot spot. If you do go, you'll find great skiing and snowboarding, the Armstrong Nugget (five pounds of pure gold) displayed at a local bank, and Barley Brown's, which has perfected the art of the India pale ale.

That wasn't the plan, however. In 1974, Brown's family was cruising from Connecticut to Seattle when the car broke down. Charmed by Baker City, they stayed, bought and ran an old bakery, then switched gears to Mexican food—"until a family of Mexicans came to town and put us out of the Mexican restaurant business."

In 1998, Brown rebuilt the eatery as a four-barrel brewpub, but beers like a Bavarian-style Hefeweizen proved a hard sell. "Everybody would say, 'Oh my God, something is wrong with that beer.' We got accused of using banana extract." The brewery's break came when they started making Tumble Off Pale Ale (medium body, decently bittered, Amarillo and Cascade) for a local ski hill. Locals started packing the brewpub nightly for dinner and WFO, their first

IPA (Magnum, Cascade, Simcoe). "I grew up racing motorcycles, and 'W.F.O.' is wide fucking open," Brown says. "We decided to throw hops all over the place and see what works."

Brown and then–head brewer Shawn Kelso drove to Idaho and Yakima Valley hop fields. "That gave us a big advantage," says Brown. Medals slowly stacked up for Tumble Off and WFO, plus the inky and strong Turmoil Cascadian Dark Ale and Tank Slapper Double IPA, which features a turbo boost of citrus and pine. Success led Brown to buy an old grocery store nearby, which he turned into a 20-barrel brewhouse. Around that time, Kelso left for 10 Barrel, but new brewer Eli Dickison couldn't start for a few months. Marks Lanham wanted a temporary gig before starting at Denver's Comrade (page 95) and created Pallet Jack, which rides a razor's edge of tropical fruit, citrus, and pine with just enough crystal malt to keep everything grounded. Pallet Jack took gold at the Great American Beer Festival in 2013, the same year that Barley Brown's was named Very Small Brewing Company of the Year.

"Locals don't care about medals," says Brown. "It's just something you hang on a wall." What matters is the freshness. "There is no such thing as old Pallet Jack anywhere in Portland. Our distributor has only five days of inventory. We fill the kegs Sunday afternoon and Monday, and they're in Portland Tuesday afternoon."

🌾 TOTAL DOMINATION

NINKASI BREWING COMPANY | ABV: 6.7%

EUGENE, OREGON | AVAILABLE: YEAR-ROUND

NINKASIBREWING.COM | GLASS: 🍺 | BITTERNESS: ★★☆☆

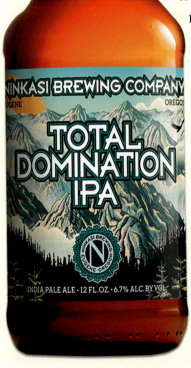

Jamie Floyd first flipped burgers for Steelhead Brewing, transitioning later to making beer. After a decade there, he opened Ninkasi, named for the Sumerian goddess of brewing. Since 2006, Ninkasi has become one of the Pacific Northwest's fastest-growing breweries, thanks to beers like Oatis, an oatmeal stout, and bitter winners like Dawn of the Red and the floral, caramel-rich Tricerahops Double IPA. In the portfolio, Total Domination does just that. It's a richly toasty amber foray into the pleasures of pine and grapefruit with citrus-rind bitterness.

FUN FACT: Ninkasi brewed Ground Control, an imperial stout flavored with hazelnuts, star anise, and cocoa nibs and fermented with ale yeast, which was launched into space.

⸎ GIGANTIC IPA

GIGANTIC BREWING | ABV: 7.3%
PORTLAND, OREGON | AVAILABLE: YEAR-ROUND
GIGANTICBREWING.COM | GLASS: 🍺 | BITTERNESS: ★★☆☆

In 2008, I met Van Havig, Rock Bottom's then–head brewer in Portland, on a brewers beer-and-bike outing. I kept tabs on his career, cheering when he and Hopworks brewer Ben Love later founded Gigantic Brewing. Their philosophy is both focused and far-ranging; they specialize in seasonals and one-offs, such as the Ume Umai, made with plums and black rice, and the Superbad Coffee Imperial Stout. The two constants, though, are IPAs: the imperial-strength, citrus-juicy Ginormous and Gigantic, a medley of orange, grapefruit, and pine drizzled with caramel, that, in their words, "continuously embiggens with each drink."

IPA ITINERARY
⇒ OREGON ⇐

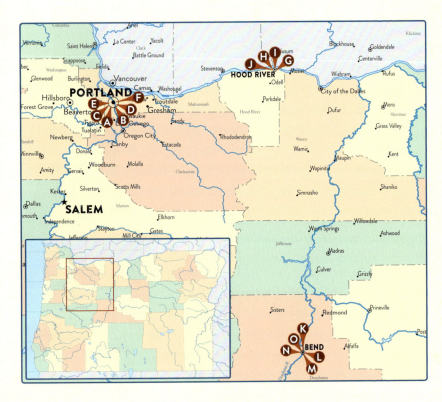

For the latest info about Oregon's breweries, visit oregoncraftbeer.org.

DAY 1: PORTLAND

Layer down, and at **BAERLIC BREWING** Ⓐ (2235 SE 11th Ave., baerlicbrewing
.com) order Invincible, their take on the classic Pacific Northwest IPA, and the
full-bodied Oatmeal Pilsner. Cross the Willamette to **OLD TOWN PIZZA AND
BREWING** Ⓑ (226 NW Davis St., oldtownpizza.com), in the historic Merchant

Hotel above the infamous Shanghai Tunnels, and sip the single-hop Revolver Pale Ale and English-leaning Shanghai'd IPA, the 2015 GABF gold medalist. On to **ECLIPTIC** **C** (825 N. Cook St., eclipticbrewing.com), for the tropical Pollux Imperial IPA and flavor-blasted Hypernova Triple IPA. A mile northeast at **HOPWORKS BIKEBAR** **D** (3947 N. Williams Ave., hopworksbeer.com), drink the IPX IPA (hops vary) and Hopworks IPA on nitro and draft. Go to **GREAT NOTION BREWING** **E** (2204 NE Alberta St. #101, greatnotionpdx.com), and sip their New England–style IPAs: island-worthy Ripe and creamy, peachy Juice Box Double IPA. Conclude at **BREAKSIDE** **F** (820 NE Dekum St., breakside.com) with dry-hopped sour La Tormenta, the pungent Wanderlust IPA, and the piney-tropical flagship IPA.

DAY 2: HOOD RIVER

Start at **DOUBLE MOUNTAIN** **G** (8 4th St., doublemountainbrewery.com) with the rich India red ale, dry-hopped Vaporizer Pale Ale, and righteously resinous and citrusy Hop Lava IPA. Stroll to **FULL SAIL** **H** (506 Columbia St., fullsailbrewing.com), and order their namesake IPA, appealingly malty and full of Centennial hops, and the citrusy and zesty Slipknot IPA. Then hoof it to **PFRIEM FAMILY BREWERS** **I** (707 Portway Ave Suite 101, pfriembeer.com) for diverse IPAs starring Mosaic, Australian cultivars, and rye. Finish at **LOGSDON BARREL HOUSE & TAPROOM** **J** (101 4th St., farmhousebeer.com) for superlative farmhouse-style saisons.

DAY 3: BEND

The trek to this high-desert city is worth it. **DESCHUTES BREWERY & PUBLIC HOUSE** **K** (1044 NW Bond St., deschutesbrewery.com) serves great IPAs, including Pinedrops and Fresh Squeezed, and brewpub specialties featuring, say, passion fruit. Continue south to **BONEYARD BEER** **L** (37 NW Lake Pl., boneyardbeer.com) and rev up with the pale, citrus-charged RPM IPA, pungent Hop-a-Wheelie, and octane-hiding Notorious Triple IPA. Shift gears to **CRUX FERMENTATION PROJECT** **M** (50 SW Division St., cruxfermentation.com), and try the Half Hitch, an imperial IPA mobbed with Mosaic, and the melony Cast Out. AB InBev now owns **10 BARREL** **N** (1135 NW Galveston Sve., 10barrel.com), but the Apocalypse IPA still hits those Pacific Northwest notes of pine, bread, and citrus. Also a must-drink: their Joe IPA. Call it a crawl at **BEND BREWING COMPANY** **O** (1019 NW Brooks St., bendbrewingco.com) with the Hop-Head Imperial IPA, and banish the day's hops with the refreshing acid of the Ching Ching Berliner Weisse.

ORBITER IPA

ECLIPTIC BREWING | ABV: 7.4%
PORTLAND, OREGON | AVAILABLE: YEAR-ROUND
ECLIPTICBREWING.COM | GLASS: 🍺 | BITTERNESS: ★★☆☆

John Harris's name might not ring a bell, but his beers should. In Deschutes's infancy, he developed Mirror Pond Pale Ale and Black Butte Porter before moving to Full Sail, where, in 1994, he brewed their first IPA. These days, Harris controls his own solo-brewing universe, the space-focused Ecliptic Brewing, where he makes flavorful constellations, such as the unfiltered Spica Pilsner, Azacca-hopped Phobos Red Ale, and the Orbiter IPA. A star chart of C-hops (Columbus, Cascade, Chinook, Centennial) creates a stellar IPA—citrus zest, pine, and biscuits with a sprinkle of sugar.

🌾 CRIKEY IPA

REUBEN'S BREWS | ABV: 6.8%

SEATTLE, WASHINGTON | AVAILABLE: YEAR-ROUND

REUBENSBREWS.COM | GLASS: 🍺 | BITTERNESS: ★★☆☆

Barely a month after Grace Robbings had son, Reuben, she bought her English-expat husband, Adam, a homebrew kit for his birthday. Adam fell hard for brewing, and in 2012 the couple birthed Reuben's Brews, which ranges across numerous styles, including cream ales, robust porters, goses, brown ales, and a kölsch as fine as anything in Cologne. Tarnished gold and topped with an off-white head, the Crikey IPA boasts a bready spine supporting notes of pine, grass, and citrus that the whole family will love.

BREWERY SPOTLIGHT

MICROBREWERY LE CASTOR | RIGAUD, QUÉBEC 🇨🇦

Murray Elliott and Daniel Addey-Jibb were apprenticing as timber framers in Scotland when they fell beneath beer's spell, daydreaming about starting a brewery. The Great Recession rocked their construction firm, and they spent their newfound free time brewing, eventually turning that passion into Le Castor in 2012. Their wild, dry-hopped formulations include Farmhouse Houblon, a Citra-hit hefeweizen, and the pleasantly piney India Session Ale.

DRINK: Yakima IPA, a citrusy, flowery ode to Pacific Northwest hop fields.

DOUBLE & TRIPLE IPAS

Over the last decade-plus, the IPA category has fostered a global game of one-upmanship as brewers formulate beers ever stronger, ever more bitter, ever more citric and resinous, but the bitterness divides. When drinkers first meet one of these gloriously bittersweet IPAs, one of two reactions happens: "That's terrible!" or "Shut up, take my money, and bring me more!" Today's IPAs have become exultations of excess, gaudy with flavors and aromas worthy of a stage revue. The modern IPA may not specialize in understatement, but it does have boundary-defying popularity and sobriety-ravaging multiples.

The double IPA bitterly defies mainstream lagers, liquid proof that beer needn't phone it in. These beers harmonize with intensely flavored food, going head-to-head with blue cheese and sharp cheddar, counterbalancing burgers, salmon, grilled game, and BBQ. As ABVs and IBUs climbed, the media gawked (guilty!) at extremes and extravagances. Mikkeller made a beer with a theoretical 1000 IBUs, while BrewDog freeze-distilled their Sink the Bismarck four times to create a quadruple IPA clocking in at 82 proof. Gimmicky, sure, but admit it: You want to try it.

It's easy to make a beer bitter to hide its flaws; it's hard to make a great bitter beer without any. The best of these beefcake IPAs nimbly toe slacklines among sweetness, bitterness, and strength—no easy feat. The more hops that go into a beer, the more brewers need to add calibrating, alcohol-boosting malt, and the greater the potential for disaster. The worst doubles or triples tumble into a muddled saccharine mess. Imagine a bitter sumo wrestler landing on your tongue.

The multiples are here to stay, but as always brewers are altering their approaches. In the hands of America's Northeast brewers, double IPAs can run milkshake-smooth, banning bitterness and embracing hops' hurriance-force perfume. Triples and quadruples do a better job of dampening the boozy burn. Whichever you prefer, seek out these IPAs, and sip them on the double—or more.

The designation "imperial" harks back to the Russian imperial stout, brewed for that country's imperial court. For linguistic variety, the terms *double* and *imperial* appear interchangeably.

⚡ DOUBLE IPAS ⚡

On herd-driven online ratings sites, such as Beer Advocate and Rate Beer, the highest scores often go to the imperials, stouts and especially IPAs. Skyscraping ratings for Lawson's Finest Liquids' Sip of Sunshine and the Alchemist's Heady Topper pique curiosity, ignite yearning, and create long lines for limited releases.

History has no shortage of beers featuring heroic amounts of hops. Take porter, for example. But the modern double IPA came to life in 1994. Vinnie Cilurzo was working at the now-shuttered Blind Pig Brewery in Temecula, California, making their flagship IPA. For the brewery's anniversary, he doubled the hop bill and cranked the malt to around 30 percent, aging the beer on oak chips and dry hops for a year. (The 100-gallon canisters, formerly owned by Knott's Berry Farm, once contained Coca-Cola syrup.) Called Inaugural Ale and presented at the 1995 Great American Beer Festival, the 120 IBU behemoth dazzled. "It was like licking the rust off a tin can!" Cilurzo told *First We Feast*. It laid the bitter foundation for Cilurzo's star-making Pliny the Elder (page 138), brewed in 2000 at Russian River, where he remains brewmaster.

Today's double IPAs boost brewery fortunes both online and in person, and they also align with flavors of fried chicken and other intense fare, such as lip-tingling Thai, Mexican, and Indian, as well as pungent cheeses and rich desserts like crème brûlée and carrot cake—trust me.

PLINY THE ELDER

RUSSIAN RIVER BREWING CO. | ABV: 8%
SANTA ROSA, CALIFORNIA | AVAILABLE: YEAR-ROUND
RUSSIANRIVERBREWING.COM | GLASS: 🍺🍷 | BITTERNESS: ★★☆☆

There comes a point in every IPA drinker's life when you must discuss Pliny the Elder. No, not the Roman naturalist who died in the A.D. 79 eruption of Mount Vesuvius, but the beer that Russian River founders Vinnie and Natalie Cilurzo named for him. Centennial, Simcoe, and Amarillo demilitarized with Columbus, Tomahawk, and Zeus conspire to create an even-keeled yet intense brew, like a couple of teaspoons of sugar lost in a pine forest. "When Natalie and I opened the pub in 2004, we made Pliny the Elder a year-round beer," says Vinnie. "Before that, it was just a seasonal beer dating back to 1999. Little by little, it picked up a near cultlike following. We knew we were brewing more over time, but it was a slow, organic growth. We were so wrapped up in the day-to-day of the business that we really had no idea what was going on with beer enthusiasts' growing fascination." Their modesty aside, this is a standard-bearer, disappearing from shelves as soon as it hits them. Drink it when you see it, but don't blow your top if you miss a bottle. This double IPA isn't bowing out anytime soon.

HOP JUJU IMPERIAL IPA

FAT HEAD'S BREWERY | ABV: 9.5%

MIDDLEBURGH HEIGHTS, OHIO | AVAILABLE: WINTER

FATHEADSBEERS.COM | GLASS: | BITTERNESS: ★★★☆

Coastal breweries dominate the conversation about America's top IPAs, often shutting out so-called fly-over country, but Fat Head's is a bona fide powerhouse, garlanded with medals for Bone Head Imperial Red, fresh-hopped Trail Head Pale Ale, and Head Hunter, a West Coast–style IPA socked with pine and grapefruit. Great American Beer Festival judges twice named Hop JuJu the country's best imperial IPA. The secret? A five-pronged hop attack (Citra, Centennial, Chinook, Cascade, Simcoe) resulting in a doggedly resinous, cleanly bitter IPA sticky with citrus and tropical fruit.

"Many people just smack the kettle with hop pellets," says Matt Cole, Fat Head's brewmaster. "We make sure at the end of the boil that we incorporate our wort with a percentage of unadulterated whole-flower hops that gives you the true natural characteristics of the hops. We try to get as much of the natural, essential oils as possible. That helps drives the flavors and aromas into the beer. We want the wow factor."

—Matt Cole, brewmaster,
Fat Head's Brewery

🌾 HEADY TOPPER

THE ALCHEMIST | ABV: 8%

STOWE, VERMONT | AVAILABLE: YEAR-ROUND

ALCHEMISTBEER.COM | GLASS: 🥫 | BITTERNESS: ★★☆☆

First brewed in 2003, the Alchemist's unfiltered flagship quickly redefined double IPAs, its blend of British barley and six top-secret hops magically conjuring pine trees, tropical fruit, and grapefruit without bitterness. It set the template for the smooth, flavorful, low-bitterness Vermont-style IPA, becoming one of America's most desired beers. "I've never been comfort-

able with the idea of laying stake to a style," Alchemist cofounder John Kimmich told *Men's Journal.* "It's just a different take and still an IPA no matter how you make it." Getting Heady ain't always easy, but it's always worth it. (Their Focal Banger IPA is also banging.)

FUN FACT: The Great American Beer Festival recognized the double IPA as a category in 2003.

In 2011, Hurricane Irene tore across the Northeast, deluging the Alchemist's original seven-barrel brewpub. The brewery moved to new digs, and one of the Northeast's top beer restaurants, Prohibition Pig, which also operates a nearby brewery, moved into the old Alchemist space.

⚜ SIP OF SUNSHINE

LAWSON'S FINEST LIQUIDS | ABV: 8%
WARREN, VERMONT | AVAILABLE: YEAR-ROUND
LAWSONSFINEST.COM | GLASS: 🍺🍷 | BITTERNESS: ★★☆☆

Sean Lawson brewed his first beer, a maple wheat ale, back in 1990 as a University of Vermont undergrad. In 2008, after a stint out west, he and wife, Karen, opened a nanobrewery that released Maple Nipple, filled with the state's famous syrup, and Sugarhouse IPA, filled with Summit and Amarillo hops. Since then, beers brewed proudly with Green Mountain ingredients (Red Spruce Bitter, Maple Triple brewed with sap and syrup instead of water) and bright, juicy, tropical IPAs have become their calling card. Triple Sunshine and the Kiwi Double IPA are nearly impossible to find, so crack open Sip of Sunshine, which Lawson brews at Connecticut's Two Roads. This floral and fruity, multi-layered brew, in Lawson's own words, tastes like a "tropical vacation in a glass."

FUN FACT: Lawson serves as resident naturalist for Mad River Glen Cooperative, leading snowshoe treks partnered with beer tastings and dinners.

🌾 HOP ZOMBIE

EPIC BREWING COMPANY | ABV: 8.5%

AUCKLAND, NEW ZEALAND | AVAILABILE: YEAR-ROUND

EPICBEER.COM | GLASS: 🍺🍷 | BITTERNESS: ★★★☆

"Prior to mid-2008, there weren't any modern-day, American-style IPAs in New Zealand," notes Epic founder Luke Nicholas. Inspired by trips to California breweries, Nicholas conquered that deficiency with grapefruit-pummeled Armageddon IPA (UK malt + US hops), regularly ranked one of the globe's best since first bottled in 2009. Epic—no relation to the Utah outfit of the same name—has kept pedal to pungent metal with single-hopped "One Trick Pony" IPAs, session-strength Imp, and double IPAs such as the super-resinous Lupulingus and Hop Zombie. Brought to life in 2011, this imperial IPA thrives on covert American and New Zealand hops evoking mangos and a medley of citrus. It's balanced and bitter without a ferocious bite.

NEBUCHADNEZZAR IMPERIAL IPA

OMNIPOLLO | ABV: 8.5%

STOCKHOLM, SWEDEN | AVAILABLE: YEAR-ROUND

OMNIPOLLO.COM | GLASS: 🍷 | BITTERNESS: ★★★☆

"Our ambition is to change the perception of beer—forever," founders Henok Fentie and Karl Grandin state grandly on the brewery's website. Fentie brews, Grandin creates the graphic labels, and the pair are reshaping Sweden's lager-dominated landscape with pulse-quickening, visually arresting concoctions, such as the subtly piney, grapefruit-driven Mazarin Pale Ale and the Nebuchadnezzar Imperial IPA, named after a Babylonian king. Developed from a homebrew recipe, it rules with a heavy hand of hops, resulting in a citrus-forward beer emphasizing flavor and drinkability over tongue-wrecking bitterness.

FUN FACT: Omnipollo's Karl Grandin cofounded the Cheap Monday clothing line.

DIRTWOLF

VICTORY BREWING COMPANY | ABV: 8.7%

DOWNINGTON, PENNSYLVANIA | AVAILABLE: YEAR-ROUND

VICTORYBEER.COM | GLASS: 🍷 | BITTERNESS: ★★★☆

In 1996, buddies Ron Barchet and Bill Covaleski turned a former Pepperidge Farm factory into Victory Brewing, anticipating the IPA craze with the deliciously impudent HopDevil, piney and spicy, sticky with caramel, and bitter as an also-ran. Victory refuses to rest on its laurels, though, using its trademark whole-flower hops in the aromatic and enlivening Vital, fruity-juicy Hop Ranch Imperial IPA, and Moving Parts, a perpetually tweaked IPA. The golden, cleanly bitter DirtWolf—pungent with pine and earth, bright with citrus and tropical fruit—references hops' scientific name, and it's one of the best big-bang-for-your-buck IPAs out there. (Also worth noting: Their Prima Pils is one of the world's top extravagantly hopped pilsners.)

"When I designed the HopDevil logo, I put lots of color into it because of the same reason that South American tree frogs use bright colors as a warning. I wanted the Coors Light drinker to look at this bottle and say, 'No way will I drink this!'"

—Bill Covaleski, cofounder, Victory Brewing

HOP-15

PORT BREWING CO. | ABV: 10%

SAN MARCOS, CALIFORNIA | AVAILABLE: MARCH AND AUGUST

PORTBREWING.COM | GLASS: 🍷🍷 | BITTERNESS: ★★★☆

Headquartered in Stone's original building, Port sets the bar for flavor-elevated SoCal IPAs, including fresh-hopped High Tide, dry and citrus-forward Wipeout, and Hop-15, originally brewed in 2002 at Pizza Port's Solana Beach location to celebrate its fifteenth anniversary. Made with a hop-secret mixture of 15 American and European varieties added every 15 minutes, this imperial IPA pours a grippingly resinous eddy of aroma and flavor that finishes with prominent citrus and pine supplied by Simcoe and Centennial in both late addition and dry-hopping. Port Brewing's portfolio also includes Lost Abbey, a line of Belgian-inspired, high-end ales, and the seasonal Hop Concept line.

FUN FACT: Port Brewing cofounders and siblings Vince and Gina Marsaglia also own the Pizza Port family of brewpubs.

BREWERY FOCUS

MELVIN BREWING, JACKSON, WYOMING | MELVINBREWING.COM

Jeremy Tofte's grandpa worked for bootlegger Al Capone, his dad toiled for Miller's and Hamm's, and he started homebrewing at nineteen, daydreaming of starting his own brewpub. In his early twenties, he dropped into Jackson to snowboard and pay for passes with restaurant gigs. When a local eatery went kaput, Tofte spent six months convincing the landlord to let him take the space, which he turned into a Thai joint. Running Thai Me Up proved rewarding, but he had beer in his blood. He sold the restaurant and brought his ambitions to New Zealand, where the beer culture wasn't quite right. Tofte was surfing away his disappointment in Indonesia when the landlord emailed. The new owners had wrecked the place. Did he want it back? "I thought people would be like, 'Oh, Jeremy's back in town, everything's awesome again,' " he recalls, but the damage was too severe. He sold his Mercedes station wagon, bought a 20-gallon brewing system, and talked friend and Pizza Port veteran Kirk McHale into joining him.

"The first two recipes that we came up with were the IPA and 2x4," Tofte recalls. "Everyone was making beer from the 1800s, and we were making the beers from the future." Tofte wisely put their IPAs on tap alongside the best beer available in Wyoming. "The ten locals who knew what we were doing started drinking every last drop." Tofte wangled a bank loan, upgraded to a three-barrel system, and McHale became head brewer. Serious experimentation followed. "Once we started perfecting 2x4, we were like, 'This is all we ever want to drink.' "

The brewery's name pays homage to their first IPA, named after a friend's drawing of an elephant—according to one explanation, that is. "I was brewing and bartending," Tofte says, "and I thought it'd be funny if people ordered a Melvin"—a wedgie variant. "We tell nice old ladies that it was an elephant," he laughs. Elephant or otherwise, Melvin has garnered fame for its intensely fruity flagship IPA, Hubert MPA (Melvin Pale Ale), and 2x4 Double IPA, which has won gold at every major beer competition, starting with the 2012 Great American Beer Festival, where it *and* the IPA both grabbed gold. "It was so quiet you could hear a pin drop," Tofte says. "People were like, 'Who the hell are they?' "

In 2016, Melvin opened a production brewery that distributes to California, Washington, and Alaska. "I always joke that IPAs are just a fad, but I'll never stop drinking them," Tofte says. "They're so freaking good."

⚜ SECOND FIDDLE

FIDDLEHEAD BREWING COMPANY | ABV: 8.2%

SHELBURNE, VERMONT | AVAILABLE: YEAR-ROUND

FIDDLEHEADBREWING.COM | GLASS: 🍷 | BITTERNESS: ★★☆☆

Matt Cohen cut his teeth at Vermont's the Shed before moving to Magic Hat. He steadily worked his way to head brewer, helping fashion the fruity #9 and Blind Faith IPA. "It was 35 IBUs. Today, it wouldn't even be considered a pale ale," he admits. At his solo brewery, opened in 2011, his unmistakable IPAs, such as the fruity Fiddlehead IPA and tropical Mastermind Double IPA, play that soft, approachable Northeast IPA chord. (His Brett beers also deserve mention.) But folks line up in droves for the succulent Second Fiddle, a canned double IPA that sounds out a creamy crescendo of mangos, peaches, and citrus from a monthlong dry-hopping spell. "It'll be 10 below, and we'll have 300 people lined up on can-release days," he says.

DREADNAUGHT

3 FLOYDS BREWING CO. | ABV: 9.5%

MUNSTER, INDIANA | AVAILABLE: YEAR-ROUND

3FLOYDS.COM | GLASS: 🍷🍷 | BITTERNESS: ★★★☆

Founded in 1996 by dad, Mike, and sons, Simon and Nick, 3 Floyds aimed to bring extreme brews to a milquetoast Midwest lager world. "Scorched earth is our brewery policy," they say, and they mean it. For two decades, they've released palate stompers such as the Dark Lord Imperial Stout, intense Arctic Panzer Wolf Imperial IPA, and Permanent Funeral Double IPA in league with grindcore band Pig Destroyer. They do lower ABVs and flavors well, too, though, notably orangey Gumballhead Wheat Ale and Citra-intensified Zombie Dust Pale Ale. Dreadnaught offers a great example of a malt-guided double IPA, its caramel base stacked with peaches and grapefruits stuck together with resin.

If imperial stouts rock your world, score a ticket to 3 Floyds' Dark Lord Day, the metal-music festival celebrating the release of their colossally flavored Russian imperial stout.

G-BOT

NEW ENGLAND BREWING CO. | ABV: 8.8%

WOODBRIDGE, CONNECTICUT | AVAILABLE: YEAR-ROUND

NEWENGLANDBREWING.COM | GLASS: 🍷 | BITTERNESS: ★★☆☆

A 2014 lawsuit in India slapped this scrappy brewery—maker of Gandhi-Bot IPA, hazy orange, hugely flavored, restrainedly bitter, citrus-ripe, exotically tropical—with the charge of defaming the memory of Mohandas Gandhi by imagining him as a robot. (It probably didn't help that Gandhi was a teetotaler.) The brewery apologized, changed the beer's name, and redid the label to depict a robotic arm flashing the peace sign amid a pile of scrap

metal and winding hop bines. If you can't find G-Bot, go for Sea Hag, one of America's earliest canned IPAs.

FUN FACT: G-Bot wasn't NEBC's first legal scrape. Lucasfilm's IP lawyers issued a cease-and-desist letter over their Imperial Stout Trooper, which featured the iconic helmet from the Star Wars franchise. New England's response? Add a fake nose, glasses, eyebrows, and mustache.

ON THE WINGS OF ARMAGEDDON

DC BRAU BREWING COMPANY | ABV: 9.2%
WASHINGTON, D.C. | AVAILABLE: YEAR-ROUND
DCBRAU.COM | GLASS: 🍷🍷 | BITTERNESS: ★★☆☆

When DC Brau opened in 2011, it became the first production brewery to operate in Washington, D.C., since 1956. On December 21, 2012—when the Mayan calendar ended but the world didn't—DC Brau celebrated the potential apocalypse with On the Wings of Armageddon, an imperial IPA soaring with Falconer's Flight, the proprietary pellet that's everything you love about Pacific Northwest hops. Canned and gently carbonated, OTWOA smells of biscuits slathered in grapefruit jam while the malted wheat helps the head hang around and smooths out the burn. The bitterness, on the other hand, will endure long past Judgment Day—if and when it arrives.

FUN FACT: The District of Columbia stands outside the three-tier system that obliges shops and bars to buy beer from wholesalers, who source it from breweries or importers. In Washington City, retailers can sell any beer they can find.

🌾 KING SUE

TOPPLING GOLIATH BREWING CO. | ABV: 8%

DECORAH, IOWA | AVAILABLE: ROTATING

TGBREWS.COM | GLASS: 🍺🍷 | BITTERNESS: ★★☆☆

Like so many others, this brewery developed from garage homebrewing. "I got sick of traveling an hour to buy my beer," Clark Lewey told the *Chicago Tribune* of his decision to brew pale ales and IPAs. In time, Clark and wife, Barb, opened a nanobrewery that fast acquired online acclaim for Citra-powered PseudoSue Pale Ale and Golden Nugget, made with Golden Promise malt and Nugget hops. Toppling's Hop Patrol series (anointed a "palate rescue mission") allows the brewery to fiddle with the latest and greatest techniques and cultivars in brews such as the Mosaic-packed Pompeii IPA and experimental XHops pale ales. Redolent of island fruit, King Sue—nickname of the biggest, best preserved *T. rex* ever found—is their supercharged, unfiltered, easy-drinking sibling.

To meet demand, Toppling Goliath partnered with Florida's
Brew Hub, a contract operation that helps breweries
meet or increase production without heavy expenditures.
Expect to see more of this model in years to come.

🌾 RED BETTY IMPERIAL IPA

CENTRAL CITY BREWERS + DISTILLERS | ABV: 9%
SURREY, BRITISH COLUMBIA | AVAILABLE: YEAR-ROUND
CENTRALCITYBEER.COM | GLASS: 🍷🍷 | BITTERNESS: ★★☆☆

Central City began in 2003 as a brewpub in a mall, originally calling this IPA Red Racer before a legal dustup with Bear Republic—makers of Red Rocket Ale and Racer 5 IPA—forced the change to Betty in America. (The brand retains its Racer name in Canada.) Either way, Central City's Red line offers one of North America's top families of IPAs, from the fruity India session ale to the flowery, citrusy IPA tuned with toffee and crystalline sweetness. Thick and lustrous, this double blends nutty and rich British Maris Otter malt with tangerine and peaches from whole-flower Pacific Northwest hops. You can sum up the border-smudging mash-up in a single word: yum.

FUN FACT: Central City also makes Hopping Mad hard ciders, including a dry-hopped version, and distills Seraph Vodka from British Columbia malted barley.

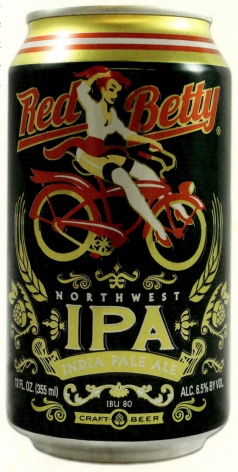

🌾 SNAKE HANDLER

GOOD PEOPLE BREWING COMPANY | ABV: 10%

BIRMINGHAM, ALABAMA | AVAILABLE: ROTATING

GOODPEOPLEBREWING.COM | GLASS: 🍷🍺 | BITTERNESS: ★★★☆

If you like session beers, you would've loved living in Alabama before 2009. Persnickety Prohibition-era laws prevented the sale of beers stronger than 6 percent ABV, which hamstrung the state's brewing scene. Legislators came to their senses, and breweries have grown like kudzu, perhaps none as much as Good People. When the brewery sold its first batch of Brown Ale (ABV: 5.4%) in 2008, it was one of the state's two production breweries. After carefully toeing the line with their Coffee Oatmeal Stout (ABV: 6%) and Pale Ale (ABV: 5.8 %), the good people at Good People have gone strong with their herbal, unfiltered IPA and West Coast–influenced Hitchhiker IPA. Their most popular offering—one of the South's choicest imperials—is Snake Handler, a pithy bite of citrus and pine covered with a caramel-smoothed malt soother.

🌾 REBEL RAW

SAMUEL ADAMS | ABV: 10%

BOSTON, MASSACHUSETTS | AVAILABLE: YEAR-ROUND

SAMUELADAMS.COM | GLASS: 🍷🍷 | BITTERNESS: ★★☆☆

Many highly rated, highly coveted double IPAs are nearly impossible to procure, relegated to brewery-only releases and scant distribution. Breathlessly unspooled on beer rating websites, word of their glory spreads like

a fable. Imagine, then, if a new-breed double IPA, short on bitterness and extreme on flavor, were available to the masses. Rebel Raw is just that. It's also the most intense and perishable member of its Rebel IPA clan. It has a 35-day sell-by date, around the standard that Stone set with its Enjoy By series. In the glass, the dark-gold nectar pours overcast, festooned with fine, slowly disappearing foam. The scent evokes the appealingly familiar formula of Pacific Northwest pine trees, primo weed, grapefruit, and tropical fruit. Taste-wise, Raw is truth in advertising, a visceral, rocky charge of earthy dankness.

FUN FACT: Boston Beer, the parent company of Samuel Adams, also makes Twisted Tea, Angry Orchard cider, and Truly Spiked boozy seltzer.

⸙ EPIPHANY

FOUNDATION BREWING COMPANY | ABV: 8%

PORTLAND, MAINE | AVAILABLE: YEAR-ROUND

FOUNDATIONBREW.COM | GLASS: 🍷 | BITTERNESS: ★★☆☆

Graphic designer Joel Mahaffey and family physician John Bonney bonded at a homebrew club over a shared love for farmhouse beers, laying the groundwork for what became Foundation. The friends do right by rustic-modern

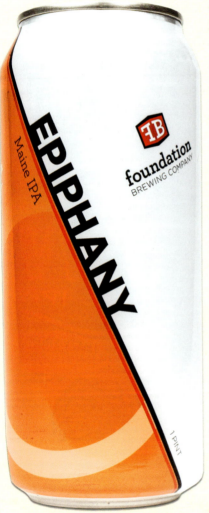

creations, such as Wanderlust, a low-ABV farmhouse ale fragrant with tropical fruit and pine, and Blaze, a citrus-fixed IPA spicy with fruity, spicy dimensions from the farmhouse yeast. Their most desirable release is Epiphany, an oat-enlivened double IPA that combines British ale yeast and American and Australian hops. Luscious and fruity, soft and citrusy, Epiphany is neither East Coast nor West Coast. No, as they say, this is a *Maine* IPA.

🌾 CAPTAIN'S DAUGHTER

GREY SAIL BREWING OF RHODE ISLAND I ABV: 8.5%
WESTERLY, RHODE ISLAND I AVAILABLE: YEAR-ROUND
GREYSAILBREWING.COM I GLASS: 🍺🍷 I BITTERNESS: ★★☆☆

Summer days spent gazing at sailboats inspired Jennifer Brinton and her homebrewer husband, Alan, to open nautically inspired Grey Sail Brewing of Rhode Island. (The wordy name resolved a trademark kerfuffle with Oregon's Full Sail.) Situated in a former macaroni factory, Grey Sail cans Flagship, a smooth cream ale with a sweet, grassy character, and Flying Jenny, an unfiltered "extra pale ale" (essentially IPA strength at 6 percent) fragrant with flowers and citrus. Their runaway hit is the cloudy Captain's Daughter, a double IPA kept light with pilsner malt, silky with oats, and tropically fruity (pineapple, mango, apricots, peaches) with Mosaic hops.

☙ WITCHSHARK IMPERIAL IPA

BELLWOODS BREWERY | ABV: 9%

TORONTO, CANADA | AVAILABLE: YEAR-ROUND

BELLWOODSBREWERY.COM | GLASS: 🍷 | BITTERNESS: ★★★☆

Opened in 2012 by several scientists-turned-brewers in one of Toronto's trendy neighborhoods, Bellwoods has become a central figure in the city's freshly ascendant beer scene. The diverse roster includes beers both barrel-aged and Belgian-inspired, plus stouts and, yes, IPAs, such as the Caribbean-worthy Roman Candle and pungent Cat Lady. The dark-orange Witchshark swoops ripe passion fruit and grapefruit across the palate with just enough toffee sweetness to stick to your taste buds. While you sip it, admire the strange label handiwork of design firm Doublenaut.

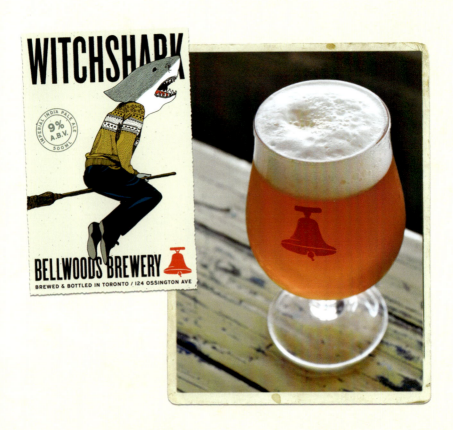

BODHI

COLUMBUS BREWING COMPANY | ABV: 8.5%

COLUMBUS, OHIO | AVAILABLE: ROTATING

COLUMBUSBREWINGCOMPANY.COM | GLASS: 🍷 | BITTERNESS: ★★☆☆

A grizzled old-timer from the class of 1988, Columbus remains a Buckeye favorite for their coppery, citrusy Pale Ale and Simcoe-hopped IPA. These days, with a larger new location and national acclaim for the dankly resinous Creeper Imperial IPA and Bodhi, the brewery is ready for a bigger share of the spotlight. Despite its heft, the Bodhi Double IPA, a golden-orange exultation of grapefruit and pine, drinks super easy without bowling you over with bitterness. Fitting for a beer named after the Buddhist concept of enlightenment.

The Columbus area has a talent for spawning great IPA breweries, also including the sassy Hoof Hearted (say it fast), mavens of the "dank and dart arts." Translation: pungent double and triple IPAs such as Roller Blabe, South of Eleven, and Dragonsaddle.

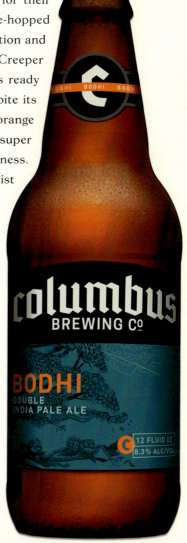

BREWERY SPOTLIGHT

BIRRIFICIO INDIPENDENTE ELAV | BERGAMO, ITALY 🇮🇹

Beginning with Grunge IPA in 2010, this brewery's unpasteurized, pull-no-punches ales veer from rosemary-added Uppercut IPA and Citra-imbued No War Rye IPA to the Humulus Black and Humulus Golden IPAs, both exclusively starring Cascade hops. They also operate several pubs and a distillery and, through their Elav Agricultural Society, grow hops, fruit, and herbs.

DRINK: Techno Double IPA, made with pale malt and Chinook and Simcoe hops.

BREWFIST | CODOGNO, ITALY 🇮🇹

Hard-hitting, hugely flavorful beers are the hallmark of this Lombard brewery. Its punchy catalog includes the imperial Czech Norris Pilsner, high-octane Green Petrol Black IPA, and Spaceman, a San Diego–worthy golden IPA over the moon with Columbus, Simcoe, and Citra.

DRINK: 2Late, an imperial IPA that, as the brewers claim, cloaks its alcohol so well that, by the time you find out it's 9.5 percent ABV, it'll be—well, you get the idea.

CERVEJARIA TUPINIQUIM | PORTO ALEGRE, BRAZIL 🇧🇷

Collaborations with A-list gypsy brewers have raised the global profile of this Brazilian brewer, which has done Saison de Caju with Stillwater (mango, cashews, wild yeast), partnered with Evil Twin on Lost in Translation Brett IPA, and contract-brews Evil Twin Brazilian beers, including Extra Fancy IPA. Lagers and fruited farmhouse ales also lie in Tupiniquim's wheelhouse.

DRINK: Polimango, a polenta-filled double IPA first brewed with Omnipollo.

KAIJU! BEER | MELBOURNE, AUSTRALIA 🇦🇺

Siblings Callum and Nat Reeves hit big with Monster Mash Double IPA and Hopped Out Red, labeled with a cartoon monstrosity, but Monster Energy drink's owners disliked the name. The brothers rebranded as Kaiju! (Japanese for "strange creature"), churning out the Cthulu on the Moon Black IPA and Betelgeuse "double red ale."

DRINK: Where Strides the Behemoth, a "double India black ale" slightly redolent of rum.

UNFILTERED BREWING | HALIFAX, NOVA SCOTIA 🇨🇦

As you might expect, brewmaster Greg Nash disdains filtration. At Unfiltered, you'll find American-style pale ales such as Hoppy Fingers, the gluten-reduced Exile on North Street IPA, All Falc'ed Up Double IPA, and Twelve Years to Zion, a double IPA north of 100 IBUs.

DRINK: Double Orange Ale, gorged with Citra and a two-row barley malt.

WAY BEER | PINHAIS, BRAZIL 🇧🇷

Established in 2010 by Alejandro Winocur and Alessandro Oliveira, Way Beer distinguishes itself with bold flavors and bold design. Galaxy hops power the American-style Die Fizzy Yellow IPA, while the Sour Me Not Berliner weisses contain native fruits like soursop.

DRINK: Double APA, twice dry-hopped and flag-waving with crystal malt and Citra and Amarillo hops.

⋇ TRIPLE & QUADRUPLE IPAS ⋇

When IPAs swell above 10 percent, the nomenclature grows fuzzier than a summer peach. These titans commonly join the ranks of the imperial realm, but a chasm of flavor, intensity, and sweetness separates a garden-variety 8 percenter from a 12 percent bruiser—territory more typical of barley wines. These weighty brews have become as commonplace as ads for light beer during a football game.

To satisfy drinkers forever wanting more, brewers continue upping the ante even though inconsistent alcohol laws mean that double-digit IPAs aren't available everywhere. As with any new trend, definitions, codified by their creators, prove slippery. Browuerij Emelisse sensibly calls its heavy-duty offering a TIPA, while Brooklyn's Sixpoint calls its Hi-Res a "IIIPA." Both beers adhere to a common 10 percent baseline for strength. Then Moylan's Hop Craic comes along at roughly the same ABV but more Roman numerals, calling itself a XXXXIPA (presumably to avoid the equally strange "IVIPA"). Founders Devil Dancer hits 12 percent but classifies itself as a triple. Farther up the ladder at 14.3 percent you'll find Valiant Brewing's Alpha Overdrive Quadruple IPA, all mango, lemons, and caramel goodness. Dogfish Head's 120 Minute IPA, a behemoth lumbering somewhere between 15 and 20 percent, avoids multiple designations altogether.

Let's set the floor for triples at 10 percent and quadruples at 12. Also note that these goliaths taste great fresh, but their alcoholic ballast ensures that they can withstand a measure of aging, turning into nightcap indulgences as their aromatics fade.

🌾 GREEN BULLET

GREEN FLASH BREWING CO. | ABV: 10.1%
SAN DIEGO, CALIFORNIA | AVAILABLE: FALL
GREENFLASHBREW.COM | GLASS: 🍷 | BITTERNESS: ★★★☆

Selecting just one great beer from every worthy brewery is bitter work, especially in the case of Green Flash, founded by husband and wife Mike and Lisa Hinkley. They make the double-strength West Coast IPA, one of California's definitive examples, the tropical standard-strength Soul Style IPA, and Le Freak, the lovechild of a Belgian tripel and imperial IPA. With Green Flash, there's no wrong IPA, but there's only one Green Bullet, a triple-strength preparation packed with New Zealand's Pacific Gem and, you guessed it, Green Bullet hops. Imagine resinous pine trees growing on a sweetly tropical isle and blowing in a bitter wind.

"Back when I started brewing professionally, there was no such thing as an American-style IPA, let alone a double or triple IPA. A few beers out there were extremely hoppy, including one that, while I was at Golden Pacific Brewing, we brewed for Hoppy Brewing called Hoppy Face Amber Ale. We nicknamed it 'Grimace Face' because it was so bitter that we assumed no one would drink it!"

—Erik Jensen, brewmaster, Green Flash Brewing Company

120 MINUTE IPA

DOGFISH HEAD CRAFT BREWED ALES | ABV: 15–20%
MILTON, DELAWARE | AVAILABLE: ROTATING
DOGFISH.COM | GLASS: 🍷 | BITTERNESS: ★★★☆

In 1999, Sam Calagione was watching a cooking show featuring a chef making soup. Adding pepper at different times created more intense flavors, which gave Calagione an idea. He bought a vibrating tabletop football game and rigged it to drop hops throughout the boil, creating the 60 Minute IPA—60 hop additions over 60 minutes of boiling. Since then, he's cranked up Dogfish Head's IPA game with the maple syrup–infused 75 Minute, 90 Minute Double, and 120 Minute, one of the indusry's strongest. First brewed in 2003, this beast boils and is hopped steadily for two hours, then it ages with additional hops for several months. The result tastes sweet, boozy, and beguilingly less bitter than you'd expect.

"I decided to call our massive (for that era) IPA an imperial IPA," Calagione says of 2001's 90 Minute. "Something like a third of our first batch was returned by distributors for being too weird, too hoppy, too expensive." Tastes have changed since then. Today 90 Minute is Amtrak's top-selling beer on Northeast and mid-Atlantic routes.

🌾 DOUBLE CROOKED TREE

DARK HORSE BREWERY | ABV: 12%

MARSHALL, MICHIGAN | AVAILABLE: FEBRUARY

DARKHORSEBREWERY.COM | GLASS: 🍷 | BITTERNESS: ★★★☆

When brewers double an IPA, they don't increase the dry ingredients two-fold because doing so would create more than just a double-strength beer. So that's just what Dark Horse did. They took their grapefruit-scented, 6.5 percent ABV Crooked Tree IPA, kept the water load the same, but added twice the grains and hops. The resulting triple-strength IPA has big bones that evoke pine and earth amid tongue-biting bitterness. It's "just the way a DOUBLE should be made," says Dark Horse, which suggests drinking it fresh or letting it age (which probably will push it closer to barley wine country). Also try their Smells Like a Safety Meeting, slang for smoking pot at work, which smells expectedly like Mary Jane working a nine-to-five.

🌾 TIPA

BROUWERIJ EMELISSE | ABV: 10%
KAMPERLAND, NETHERLANDS | AVAILABLE: YEAR-ROUND
EMELISSE.NL | GLASS: 🍷🍷 | BITTERNESS: ★★★☆

This brewpub off the Netherlands' southwestern coast takes its name from a village swept away by flooding in the 1530s, but since 2004 the folks here have expertly navigated the channels between the accessible (pilsner, blonde ale, dubbel) and the ingenious, creating their Earl Grey IPA, a marshmallow-infused stout, and the White Label series, which includes sour ales aged in ex–balsamic vinegar barrels. Similarly perched on the edge of the flavorful extreme lies the burnt orange Triple IPA, flooded with Pacific Northwest hops including Simcoe, Amarillo, and Chinook. Sticky as cotton candy, it tastes of caramel rolled in oranges, pine needles, and pineapples. Sip it slowly, and save space for their excellent BIPA (black IPA).

FUN FACT: Kees Bubberman, Emelisse's former brewmaster, now steers Brouwerij Kees, doling out the contemporary-style Mosaic Hop Explosion, Double Rye, and Pink Grapefruit IPAs.

BREWERY FOCUS

OTHER HALF BREWING, BROOKLYN, NEW YORK | OTHERHALFBREWING.COM

The plan was always to brew IPAs. Portland native Sam Richardson honed his craft at Pyramid Brewing and came to Brooklyn as head brewer for Greenpoint Beer Works, a contract outfit. There he met Matt Monahan, a chef transitioning into brewing. They bonded over a shared ardor for IPAs.

In the 1960s, Brooklyn produced 10 percent of all American beer, but as recently as 2013 the borough had only a few breweries outside Greenpoint, headlined by Brooklyn Brewery and Sixpoint. "There was just not enough production happening," says Monahan. "The second we decided to do this, we were signing hop contracts five years out." Red tape stretched the building plan from ten weeks to around seventy-five, but the slog had a silver lining. In that time, New York State passed legislation allowing taprooms to sell pints, so the partners added a bar.

Their releases, rarely repeated batch to batch, tap both the contemporary New England style (cloudy, fruity) and West Coast (dry, malt-balanced), sometimes landing in the middle. "In terms of being super-clean or fruity, we're still trying to make it super-aromatic," Richardson says. "Why limit yourself? We like variety." Which explains their successes with ESBs, imperial stouts, wild saisons fermented in oak foudres, and other experiments aged in, say, ex-Cognac casks.

A few predawn Saturdays each month, IPA acolytes—some regularly venturing from as far away as West Virginia—journey to an industrial stretch of Brooklyn's Carroll Gardens neighborhood to line up before a graffiti-scrawled warehouse for wristbands that let them buy their allotment of Other Half's latest offering. They come for single-hopped IPAs, the dank and fruity All Green Everything Triple IPA, or the dry and juicy Green Diamonds. The turnout continually amazes Richardson. "You don't open a business and go, 'You know what we're going to do? We're going to sell all these cans out of the brewery in one day, every two weeks.' "

🌾 HOP CRAIC XXXXIPA

MOYLAN'S BREWERY & RESTAURANT | ABV: 10.4%
NOVATO, CALIFORNIA | AVAILABLE: ROTATING
MOYLANS.COM | GLASS: 🍷 | BITTERNESS: ★★★★

Brendan Moylan's beer journey began in San Francisco in the late 1970s as beer manager at a local liquor store while he refined his homebrew skills. In time, he moved to import sales, which gave him an outside-in understanding of the business. In 1989, he cofounded Marin Brewing—which makes the medal-winning Marin IPA and White Knuckle Double IPA—and, later, his namesake brewery, which makes big beers, such as the Scotch-style Kilt Lifter or the resinous Moylander Double and Hopsickle Imperial IPAs. A longtime customer favorite, the rich Hop Craic (pronounced "crack") has a caramel foundation and all the tropical pine you could want. The sweetness and weighty, bitter finish ensure a languorous sip.

FUN FACT: Moylan also founded Stillwater Spirits, which distills single-malt whiskey, bourbon, rye, and vodka.

🌾 MOLOTOV COCKTAIL HEAVY

EVIL TWIN BREWING | ABV: 17.2%
BROOKLYN, NEW YORK | AVAILABLE: ROTATING
EVILTWIN.DK | GLASS: 🍷 | BITTERNESS: ★★★★

Globetrotting gypsy brewer Jeppe Jarnit-Bjergsø makes countless unique concoctions, including the sweet Imperial Doughnut Break, funkily refreshing NoMader Weisse, and eucalyptus-scented Mission Gose. The Femme Fatale Brett and its fruited variants offer great examples of the wild IPA, and the lightly tropical Citra Sunshine Slacker Session IPA is perfectly sippable. If you crave a flavor conflagration, however, the Molotov pack of elevated-alcohol IPAs is—wait for it—the bomb. Molotov Lite drinks approachably at 8.5 percent, while the chewily bitter Molotov Cocktail warms up to 13 percent. Concealing its alcohol like a lethal weapon, the belly-heating, fruity, slick Heavy is bittersweet nightcap juice.

FUN FACT: Jarnit-Bjergsø coowns Tørst, one of Brooklyn's most bespoke beer bars, which includes Luksus, a Michelin-starred restaurant.

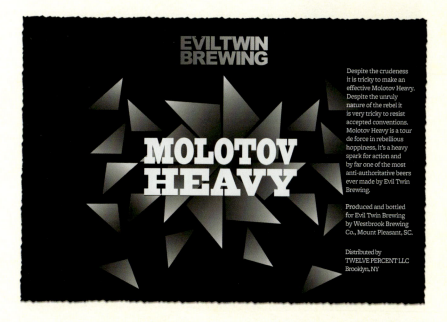

DOUBLE & TRIPLE IPAS ★ 171

HOP-DE-RANGED

KNEE DEEP BREWING COMPANY | ABV: 13.1%

AUBURN, CALIFORNIA | AVAILABLE: ROTATING

KNEEDEEPBREWING.COM | GLASS: 🍷 | BITTERNESS: ★★★★

Brandishing every conceivable pun, Knee Deep specializes in endless permutations of IPAs at nearly every ABV and with label art often featuring an anthropomorphized hop. Try their Belgo-Hoptologist Double IPA, orangey and fruity Hop Trio IPA, and Breaking Bud IPA, a dank, tropical brew honoring Walter White. The orange-gold Hop-De-Ranged—a self-described "Quad IPA that borders on insanity"—is a pungently bitter palate eradicator made of resin, citrus rind, and thick malt sweetness. Let it warm, nip it leisurely, and don't plan on doing anything meaningful afterward.

FUN FACT: Knee Deep's founding brewmaster, Jeremy Warren, started Revision Brewing, which focuses on barrel-aged beers, experimental sours, and audacious IPAs.

ⵂ HOPDOOM

NAPARBIER | ABV: 11.5%

PAMPLONA, SPAIN | AVAILABLE: YEAR-ROUND

NAPARBIER.COM | GLASS: 🍷 | BITTERNESS: ★★★☆

Bulls famously run through the streets here every sum-mer, and since 2009 brewer Juan Rodriguez has been hitting the bull's-eye of flavor. Naparbier—a portman-teau of the region ("Napar" is Basque for Navarre) and the German word for beer—makes a classic pilsner and porter as well as more adventurous fare, includ-ing an imperial stout seasoned with pumpkins and habaneros and IPAs with a keen emphasis on fresh-ness, American hops, and horror-movie names. Get a load of the Hoptopus from Outer Space and the Alien Claw IPAs. Filled with Maris Otter and crys-tal malts, the ruggedly bitter HopDoom releases a resinous stampede of pine, grapefruit, and orange peel—and that's no bull.

FUN FACT: Naparbier collaborated with Mikkeller to create We Brew Gold, an imperial IPA that, like Goldschläger, had sparkling flakes of gold in it.

🌾 HOP'SOLUTELY

FEGLEY'S BREW WORKS | ABV: 11.5%

BETHLEHEM, PENNSYLVANIA | AVAILABLE: YEAR-ROUND

THEBREWWORKS.COM | GLASS: 🍷 | BITTERNESS: ★★★★

As Bethlehem Steel, once America's biggest shipbuilder, and the fortunes of its hometown rusted away, the Fegley family fought back by opening a brewpub downtown. The establishment became a community anchor, finding success with beers such as the ESB and Valley Golden Ale. Fegley's also does well by more adventuresome beers, including Arctic Alchemy, their version of a strapping Victorian brew that fortified British voyagers to the Arctic Circle, and the Hop'solutely Triple IPA. Gassed up with pale and crystal malt and Pacific Northwest hops (Summit, Amarillo, Chinook,

and more), mouth-coating Hop'solutely has an herbal, hefty caramel-honey sweetness that supports an all-terrain battering of citrus and pine. Its steady availability also merits a gold star.

🌾 SEEK AND DESTROY

BLACK MARKET BREWING COMPANY | ABV: 12%
TEMECULA, CALIFORNIA | AVAILABLE: FEBRUARY
BLACKMARKETBREW.COM | GLASS: 🍷 | BITTERNESS: ★★★★

Sierra Nevada fan Kevin Dyer started small in 2009 with a garage-based one-barrel system brewing a Bavarian-style hefeweizen that cracked the local market for flavorful beer. His spy-themed Black Market line focuses on all strengths and hues of IPAs, including the medium-strength Aftermath, wheat-enhanced Liberation Imperial IPA, and Holiday, a "triple black rye IPA." Those make a fine segue to winter's Seek & Destroy, a quadruple featuring atypical malts smoked with cherrywood and mesquite. Laced with Columbus, Citra, and several experimental varieties, S&D drinks like you're snacking on oranges and grapefruit beside a campfire in a pine-filled wilderness.

FUN FACT: Brewer and beer consultant Randy Mosher, author of the essential *Tasting Beer* and *Radical Brewing*, also does graphic design. His clients include Black Market, Bruery, and Metropolitan Brewing.

4

SESSION IPAS

Getting drunk is simple. It's staying sober that takes skill—especially when faced with the delicious onslaught of so many IPAs. Midwestern lagers dominated the not-too-distant past, and most hovered around 5% ABV. Even early craft pioneers exercised restraint. You could drink a Sierra Nevada Pale Ale (5.6% ABV), Anchor Steam (4.9% ABV), or two and keep a clear head. Today's IPAs have a roughly 7% baseline. Just two little percent points more, right? Nope!

If a friend is knocking back an Odell 5 Barrel Pale Ale (5.2% ABV) and you're sipping an Ithaca Flower Power (7.5% ABV), you're downing nearly *50 percent more* alcohol. Stretch that over a six-pack, and you understand why my wife constantly restocks our stash of ibuprofen.

Session IPAs—so-called because, in British pub culture, you can drink several in one drinking session—marry a moderate ABV, often around 4.5 percent, with all the craveable flavors and fragrances you love in full-strength offerings. Nailing this balancing act doesn't come easy, though. The more hops you add, the more malt a beer needs for equilibrium, which gives yeast more fuel to make fire-water. Brewers solve the problem by using loads of late-addition hops, especially cultivars heavy on citrus or tropical fruit, which deliver all the aroma and taste without the enamel-scraping bitterness.

Session IPAs have become a runaway success, proving the enduring appeal of low-ABV beer. Founders All Day reigns as category king, but it has lots of company; most IPA breweries offer a riff. The IPA is now in session.

🌾 LEFT OF THE DIAL IPA

NOTCH BREWING | ABV: 4.3%

SALEM, MASSACHUSETTS | AVAILABLE: YEAR-ROUND

NOTCHBREWING.COM | GLASS: 🍺 | BITTERNESS: ★★☆☆

Long before sessions became buzzworthy, Chris Lohring tapped the drum at Notch, which he launched in 2010 with a then-radical mission to create full-flavored, low-alcohol beers. With a collection of pilsners, saisons, corn lagers, and Berliner weisses, he proved that less really is more. Left of the Dial—a coppery symphony of sweet, robust Fawcett Golden Promise malt and new-school hops, including Citra and Mosaic—will besot you; it's fruit-sweet, citrusy, and piney in all the right places.

FUN FACT: Until 2016, when the Salem location opened, Notch was a gypsy brewery.

"The best session IPAs draw on UK tradition. They achieve a low gravity with flavorful base malt, but instead of British hops they use newer varietals—more flavors and aromas of fruit, citrus, and pine but with a restrained bitterness. This combination provides a more subtle and elegant approach than chest-thumping bitterness and cloying sweetness, creating a better setup for multiple pints. Nothing in brewing is really new; we just improve on it."

—Chris Lohring, founder, Notch Brewing

🌾 SESSION IPA (11)

BREW BY NUMBERS | ABV: VARIES. GENERALLY SUB-5%

LONDON, ENGLAND | AVAILABLE: ROTATING

BREWBYNUMBERS.COM | GLASS: 🍺 | BITTERNESS: ★★☆☆

These Brits take a studied, quantitative, analytical approach to brewing, creating a stylistic parameter—saison, witbier, porter, etc.—assigning a digit, then testing numerically unique recipes. For example, 05/10 = IPA: wheat, Amarillo + Cascade. Their revolving, naturally carbonated session IPAs (#11) stand among the kingdom's best, employing higher brewing temperatures to leave enough residual sweetness to balance the ludicrous hopping rates. Equally worthy are the Citra (11/05), Mosaic (11/03), and Amarillo-Nelson (11/01).

"A session IPA should replicate a regular IPA in all aspects except one: ABV. The lack of alcohol requires additional work to ensure the beer has enough body. A warm mash increases nonfermentable sugars in the wort, leaving the finished beer richer. The use of wheat or oats also can add body to a beer. Flavor- and aroma-hop additions should be identical to regular, full-strength IPAs. Using the right hops is equally important; big aroma hops with high oil content add juiciness to the finished beer. Don't be shy about bitterness."

—Dave Seymour, cofounder, Brew by Numbers

🌾 GO TO IPA

STONE BREWING | ABV: 4.5%

SAN DIEGO, CALIFORNIA | AVAILABLE: YEAR-ROUND

STONEBREWING.COM | GLASS: 🍺 | BITTERNESS: ★☆☆☆

These Southern Californians make applause-worthy hop bombs, such as the RuinTen Triple IPA ("a stage dive into a mosh pit of hops") and the Enjoy By double IPA series, debuted in 2012 and crafted to be consumed within 37 days. When it comes to lower ABVs, "It's great to get that full hop blast without the alcohol," says former brewmaster Mitch Steele. Go To goes back to 2010, when Steele collaborated with homebrewer Kelsey McNair on the San Diego County Session Ale Steele, a 4.2 percenter. "It was like drinking a double IPA without having to worry about what you were doing when you were done drinking." The trick that both brews use is called hop-bursting, using ten hops, including Experimental Hopsteiner 06300, to create extreme aromatics rather than bitterness. The finished product packs a peachy, melony punch and just a hint of tingling bitterness.

FUN FACT: Conceived during the hop shortage of 2008, Stone's 12th Anniversary Bitter Chocolate Oatmeal Stout subbed out hops for the bitterness of unsweetened chocolate.

🌾 BOAT BEER

CARTON BREWING COMPANY | ABV: 4.2%

ATLANTIC HIGHLANDS, NEW JERSEY | AVAILABLE: YEAR-ROUND

CARTONBREWING.COM | GLASS: 🍺 | BITTERNESS: ★☆☆☆

Founder and foodie Augie Carton brain-flashes flavor-charged, eclectic, conceptual ales, including Regular Coffee, a potent cream ale that mimics milky, sweetened java; Panzanella, which evokes tomato and cucumber bruschetta; or Digger, a salted ale seasoned with lemongrass and, yep, clams. "The thing about being a brewery in a shore town is that our water, by its nature, is a salty thing," Carton says. "We don't often correct our minerals when we brew." Boat unites that unique water with German malts, kölsch yeast, and crates of American hops, creating a fizzy, grapefruit-laced crusher suited for bright-eyed brunch or last call on land or sea. If you crave stronger fare, try the resin-walloped 007XX double IPA.

⚑ BABY DADDY

SPEAKEASY ALES & LAGERS ⎮ ABV: 4.7%

SAN FRANCISCO, CALIFORNIA ⎮ AVAILABLE: YEAR-ROUND

GOODBEER.COM ⎮ GLASS: 🍺 ⎮ BITTERNESS: ★★☆☆

Cloaked in Prohibition-era mafioso noir, Speakeasy has been one of SFO's open secrets since 1997. Homebrewing founder Forest Gray launched the biz with Prohibition Ale, a hop-goosed amber, later adding other lupulin offerings: Floral Big Daddy, bouncing with grapefruit and pine, which hunkers alongside Caribbean-leaning Mosaic-hopped Metropolis Lager; and Double Daddy, thrice dry-hopped. In 2015, Speakeasy unfurled its Session 47 series, featuring invigorating Pop Gun Pilsner and Baby Daddy. This diminutive IPA goes big on lime and passion fruit aroma, but note the beer's dad bod, pleasantly bigger than expected, for a moment before reaching for a second.

MOSAIC SESSION IPA

KARL STRAUSS BREWING COMPANY | ABV: 5.5%

SAN DIEGO, CALIFORNIA | AVAILABLE: YEAR-ROUND

KARLSTRAUSS.COM | GLASS: 🍺 | BITTERNESS: ★★☆☆

Red Trolley Ale and Columbia Street Amber are rock-solid beers, but they echo an earlier era of color-coded brews. In recent years, Karl Strauss has embraced and mastered thoroughly modern styles and ingredients, rolling Citra and Simcoe through Aurora Hoppyalis, their San Diego–style IPA, and putting Mosaic front-and-center in this eponymous ale. It's a smidgen stronger than your average session IPA, but one sip of the fluffy-headed blonde belle—a lively mélange of grapefruit, blueberries, mango, and cantaloupe—and you'll let Karl slide.

Born in his dad's brewery, Karl Strauss fled Nazi Germany in 1939 and found his future in Pabst, rising to vice president of production. After he retired, cousin Chris Cramer and college roommate Matt Rattner tapped Karl's expertise. He helped start his namesake brewery in 1989, San Diego's first in more than fifty years, serving as master brewer until 2006, when he died at age ninety-four. What a brewing life!

BREWERY FOCUS

FOUNDERS BREWING, GRAND RAPIDS, MICHIGAN | FOUNDERSBREWING.COM

First known as Canal Street Brewing Company, Founders found its current identity in the early label art of a bygone brewery, the word "Founders" across the top. Their rich and malty Dirty Bastard Scotch Ale, hellaciously hopped Devil Dancer Triple IPA, and ex-bourbon KBS Imperial Stout waged war with drinkers' taste buds, a perfect tactic for the wide-open years of the new millennium. "We kind of got a reputation for our beers being big, bold, and complex," says Dave Engber, who cofounded the brewery in 1997 with friend and fellow homebrewer Mike Stevens.

The brewers fiddled with ratios, adding these malts, those hops, seeking a beer to balance bitterness, flavor, and alcohol. If you had visited the taproom in the early era, you might've sipped Solid Gold, Endurance, and Super Gold. Each trial brought them closer to All Day IPA, a brisk and brightly aromatic 4.7% ABV standout released seasonally in 2010. It rapidly resonated with drinkers seeking maximum flavor and moderate sobriety.

"We knew that it would take off, but we didn't know at what kind of accelerated rate," says Engber. In 2012, All Day became an all-year offering that captured national interest. "We didn't think we'd create an entire category for the industry," Stevens admits.

Today you can buy cans of All Day, which accounts for more than half of sales, by the 15-pack. That ratio should raise eyebrows, given Founders' pride in brand diversity, including raspberry-filled Rübæus, chocolaty Porter, and reDANKulous, an imperial red IPA. "Within a pretty short amount of time, All Day became our highest-volume brand," says Engber.

Founders still innovates; see their Mosaic Promise Pale Ale and Azacca IPA, a fruity, smooth, and sneaky-strong amalgamation. "People are screaming for aromatic hops," Engber says, "but we have to be very cautious. You don't want to have an entire portfolio of IPAs that are imperial versions of one another." So Founders tests new hop varieties and formulas, barrel-aging this and that, while All Day remains an anchor proving that flavor and low ABV aren't mutually exclusive. "It's just a pure and delicious beer," Engber says.

⚜ GUINEU RINER

CA L'ARENYS | ABV: 2.5%

BARCELONA, SPAIN | AVAILABLE: YEAR-ROUND

CALARENYS.CAT | GLASS: 🍺 | BITTERNESS: ★☆☆☆

Guineu means fox in Catalan, and the offerings made by this homebrew-supply-shop-turned-brewery feature delightful featherweights like the Sitges wheat pale ale, wild No Sucks (a joke reffing that the beer includes no *Saccharomyces* yeast), and Guineu Riner, a citrusy, unfiltered sip of perfection, light-bodied but flavorfully hopped with Amarillo. In other words, it's the ideal beer to drink by the dozen.

IPAs are limboing ever lower, Guineu Riner among them, to the 2% mark. Florida's Green Bench Brewing dropped the De Soto Low (2.3% ABV), which keeps skinny, hoppy company with Siren Half Mast QIPA (2.7% ABV), Bissell Brothers Diavoletto (2.6% ABV), and Mikkeller Drink'in the Sun, of which some batches sink all the way down to just 0.3% ABV!

❧ PINNER THROWBACK IPA

OSKAR BLUES | ABV: 4.9%

LONGMONT, COLORADO | AVAILABLE: YEAR-ROUND

OSKARBLUES.COM | GLASS: 🍺 | BITTERNESS: ★★☆☆

These cheeky, cannabis-loving Coloradans named their low-alcohol IPA after a mini joint—a session stoner if you will. As the brewery says, "It's the perfect beer for a little sip, sip, give." The golden Pinner hits with haymakers of aroma and flavor, a sensory punch of pineapples, Florida citrus, pine, and tropical fruit, but biscuits and a pleasant baseline bitterness balance the whole. If you dig stronger stuff, go for the copper-hued, stickily resinous Deviant Dale's Double IPA and the berry-licious "metamodern-style" IPA, featuring Topaz, Galaxy, and Vic Secret.

Oskar Blues, the first craft brewery to can its beer, recently invented the Crowler. Production manager Jeremy Rudolf was fiddling with a tabletop canning machine and discovered that he could retrofit it for 32-ounce cans, allowing bars and breweries to can draft beer in a single-serving, recyclable package.

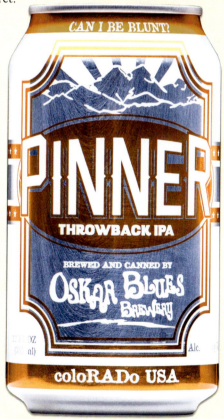

⚜ U.S. LIGHT ALES AND SESSION IPAS

CLOUDWATER BREW CO. | ABV: VARIES

MANCHESTER, ENGLAND | AVAILABLE: SPRING & SUMMER

CLOUDWATERBREW.CO | GLASS: 🍺 | BITTERNESS: ★☆☆☆

Releasing a range of beers for each half orbit of the Earth, Cloudwater focuses, in their words, on modern, seasonal beer. The fall-winter stretch brings darker beers, such as autumnal red ales, imperial stouts, and highly hopped double IPAs using the freshest hop crops. Spring and summer bring light and radiantly refreshing beers, low-strength lagers showcasing expressive British aroma hops, Vermont-inspired juicy IPAs, and a session bitter that blends American yeast and hops, British tradition, and Australian hops. The U.S. Light Ales (3.5% ABV) and Session IPAs (4.5% ABV) offer moving targets that feature choice varietals, such as Mosaic and Nelson Sauvin.

FUN FACT: The brewery's name stems from the Japanese Zen Buddhist word *unsui*, meaning "cloud, water." According to founder Paul Jones, "It's a term for a novice who has undertaken training."

In *Craft Beer World*, Mark Dredge identifies a burgeoning UK style he anoints "pale and hoppy session beer," which sits refreshingly between 3 and 4% and uses plenty of citric, fruity New World hops. "It's the combination of huge hop flavours and the quenching bitterness that best defines these beers," he writes, name-checking Moor Revival and Buxton Moor Top. Add Dark Star HopHead, and you might have the makings of a movement.

⚕ LIL' HEAVEN

TWO ROADS BREWING COMPANY | ABV: 4.8%
STRATFORD, CONNECTICUT | AVAILABLE: YEAR-ROUND
TWOROADSBREWING.COM | GLASS: 🍺 | BITTERNESS: ★★☆☆

Housed in a century-old manufacturing building, this fascinating out-fit contract-brews some of the country's most sought ales (Stillwater, Evil Twin, Lawson's Finest Liquids) and creates its own line of highly regarded elixirs, including the peppery Worker's Comp Saison, hop-rocked Ol' Factory Pils, and citrus-socked Road 2 Ruin Double IPA. Named for the crawl-space where workers napped and undertook other illicit activities, the hazy orange, slightly doughy Lil' Heaven contains a quartet of au courant hops (Azacca, Equinox, Calypso, Mosaic) that form a tropical spread of mangos, grapefruit, and pineapples.

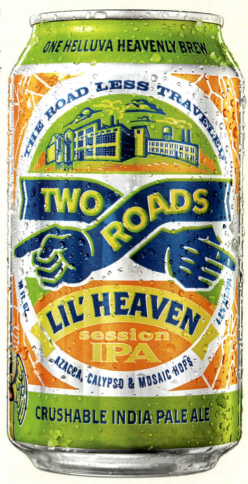

FUN FACT: Phil Markowski, brewmaster for Two Roads, wrote the book on *Farmhouse Ales*.

SARANAC GEN IV SESSION IPA

MATT BREWING COMPANY | ABV: 4.5%

UTICA, NEW YORK | AVAILABLE: SUMMER

SARANAC.COM | GLASS: 🍺 | BITTERNESS: ★★☆☆

This resilient, adaptable, family-run brewery, America's fourth oldest, has made beer since 1888. It survived Prohibition by manufacturing soft drinks and booze-free malt tonics before emerging to make Utica Club Lager. In the 1980s, Bud and Miller were battering Matt; to fight back, it launched the Saranac line in 1985, finding success with the all-malt 1888 Lager. Today, the stalwart is doubling down on heritage with on-trend, meticulously balanced releases like the Gen IV, honoring four generations of family ownership. Wheat, interlocked with caramel, supplies a smooth framework, and the rush of grapefruit and tropical fruit comes from Amarillo and Citra.

FUN FACT: Matt Brewing has contract-brewed for a number of start-ups, including stalwart Brooklyn, bygone Pete's, and ephemeral Billy Beer. Don't remember that one? It was the awful lager endorsed by the younger brother of President Carter.

TANGIER

SOUTHERN TIER BREWING COMPANY | ABV: 4.6%
LAKEWOOD, NEW YORK | AVAILABLE: YEAR-ROUND
STBCBEER.COM | GLASS: 🍺 | BITTERNESS: ★★☆☆

The boozy flights of culinary fancy that Southern Tier makes, especially fall's potent Pumking and Crème Brûlée, a dessert-inspired milk stout, still excel, but their shallower shoals have loads to offer as well, particularly summer's bright, lemony Hop Sun Wheat Ale and Tangier, a session IPA named after the Moroccan port city. Pop open the golden concoction and you'll release a citrusy perfume of tangerine peels. The light-bodied, lightly biscuity beer makes for an invigorating sipper with moderate bitterness and Azacca hops adding beguiling layers of tropical fruit.

FUN FACTS: In college, Southern Tier founder Phin DeMink homebrewed with Firestone Walker brewmaster Matt Brynildson.

TRADER SESSION IPA

UINTA BREWING COMPANY | ABV: 4%
SALT LAKE CITY, UTAH | AVAILABLE: YEAR-ROUND
UINTABREWING.COM | GLASS: 🍺 | BITTERNESS: ★★☆☆

Utah's booze laws ban brews stronger than 4% ABV from draft lines, so breweries such as Uinta have become session experts by necessity. Released on draft in 1994, Trader offered a session IPA before most drinkers had even *heard* of IPAs. This brightly lit billboard of a beer advertises Christmas pine on the tongue and, thanks to a heavy hand of Centennial hops, fresh flowers and citrus zest. Take note of the toasted malt, too.

Fellow Salt Laker Epic Brewing (page 96) makes the Utah Session series of beers, all 4% ABV or less, including a sour IPA.

TAKE 5

HARPOON BREWERY | ABV: 4.3%

BOSTON, MASSACHUSETTS | AVAILABLE: YEAR-ROUND

HARPOONBREWERY.COM | GLASS: 🍺 | BITTERNESS: ★★☆☆

Boston's modern brewing era began when Harpoon dropped anchor in 1986, clutching the commonwealth's first brewing permit in a quarter century. Five years later, Harpoon noticed that no East Coast brewer was dabbling in the West Coast's newly popular hopped-up ales. So they released their flagship IPA—English in origin, Pacific Northwest in aroma and bitterness—in 1993; it remains an enduring favorite. The Hoppy Adventure Double IPA taps the juicy, tropical vein, but fill your fridge with Take 5, which brims with piney Simcoe and citrusy Amarillo alongside Vienna and English amber malts that keep the body front and center. That combo pays delicious dividends. Take a 12-pack the next time you head to the shore.

CAMPSIDE SESSION IPA

UPLAND BREWING COMPANY | ABV: 4.5%

BLOOMINGTON, INDIANA | AVAILABLE: SPRING AND SUMMER

UPLANDBEER.COM | GLASS: 🍺 | BITTERNESS: ★★☆☆

During the last ice age, glaciers flattened southern Indiana's rolling, wooded hills, leaving behind what geologists dubbed the Uplands, which inspired this Hoosier State brewery, operating since 1997. The lineup blends approachable, easy-drinkers, such as spiced Wheat Ale and chocolatey Bad Elmer's Porter, with wild forays, including its sought-after sours fruited with kiwis, peaches, and strawberries. In the middle sits the slightly cloudy, lightly honey-sweet Campside, which kindles interest with its scaled-back bitterness and fragrant foxtrot of pine needles and grapefruit.

BREWERY SPOTLIGHT

BRASSERIE DE LA SENNE | BRUSSELS, BELGIUM 🇧🇪

Yvan de Baets and Bernard Leboucq focus on unfiltered, unpasteurized, and uncommonly multifaceted ales generously peppered with European hops and adorned with Art Deco labels, producing the engagingly malty, bitter-fruity Zinnebir, piney and chocolatey Brusseleir Zwët IPA, plus peerless stouts, saisons, and tripels.

DRINK: Taras Boulba, a grassy, lemony, yeasty-good Belgian pale ale/hoppy blonde.

CERVECERÍA ROTHHAMMER | SANTIAGO, CHILE 🇨🇱

Frustrated by the lack of likable beers in lager-loving Chile, former professional snowboarder Sebastián Rothhammer partnered with his two brothers to found this family brewery. Their lineup favors in-your-face flavors, including the 100 IBU Brutal IPA, Epic Barley Wine, and Rebel Imperial Pilsner, 9% ABV and walloped with Cascade.

DRINK: Nazca, a session IPA that weds pilsner malt to Cascade and Mosaic.

GARAGE BEER CO. | BARCELONA, SPAIN 🇪🇸

James Welsh and Alberto Zamborlin met at the brewing academy led by Steve Huxley, Iberian beer's Johnny Appleseed, and decided to open design-savvy Garage Beer. Their on-trend lineup includes the crisp and healthily hopped Riba Lager and Beast Berliner Weisse, and they have collaborated with tastemakers such as Other Half for the session In Green We Trust.

DRINK: Garage IPA, abundantly dry-hopped with Cascade and Centennial.

MASTER GAO | NANJING, CHINA 🇨🇳

Yan Gao literally wrote the book on homebrewing—in Mandarin. At his namesake facility, the guru, who formerly ran a pharmaceutical research company, makes unique beers, such as Sweet Olive Lager and Jasmine Wit. They also create their fair share of IPAs, including the session-strength Imperial River and bitter and flowery Holy Devil.

DRINK: Baby IPA, China's very first bottled IPA.

EMERGING STYLES

Restless and shape shifting, the IPA has become a palimpsest on which brewers record every inspiration and experimental desire. Starting from the simple formula of using more hops than average, the IPA has spun in dozens of unexpected directions. Today's risk-takers amplify its citrusy qualities by adding fruit, as in Ballast Point's Grapefruit Sculpin and Lagunitas's CitruSinensis. Other breweries swap ale yeast for a lager strain, fashioning brisk, well-bittered sippers, such as the Bruery's Humulus Lager, or they sub wild *Brettanomyces* for category-exploding IPAs, including Evil Twin's funky Femme Fatale Brett. Oklahoma's Prairie Artisan Ales heavily dry-hops its Funky Gold sours; Vermont's the Beanery revs its IPAs with java; and Nebraska Brewing cross-pollinates a potent Belgian tripel with a West Coast IPA, aging the amalgamation in ex-Chardonnay barrels.

Brewers will shove anything into the brew kettle, it seems, including wheat, carrots, and even habanero peppers. Where some see gimmick, I see innovation. Both consumer demand and self-differentiation are driving these radical variations on a theme. If everyone's brewing a bright, citrusy West Coast IPA, who wants yet another version of the same beer? Better to make the absolute best version out there or something tongue-tinglingly new. Not every offshoot will withstand the test of time or fickle consumer tastes. Some flashes will burn out fast. (Shock Top Wheat IPA, we barely knew ye.) Others will endure and expand the canon. Here are the keys to the bitter future.

⊱ SEASONAL ⊰

You'll find IPAs on offer 365 days of the year, exploding with flavor on the Fourth of July and warming us up as snowflakes flutter to the ground. Every day may provide a new opportunity to drink an IPA, but only the fall offers a chance to savor the bitter thrill of beers made with wet and fresh hops, the harvest bottled for your enjoyment.

WET & FRESH HOP IPAS

Let's commence in the kitchen with the marked difference between cooking with dried herbs and fresh. The former require only a minor sprinkling, while garden-fresh herbs have a green and vibrant flavor, the mark of living plant matter. Beer's not much different. Most every beer contains dried hops. Like freshly picked basil, just-harvested hops smell sublime. Within a day or two, though, degradation begins. To preserve aromatics and flavors, growers dry and pelletize them. Drying eliminates delicate volatile oils and other aromas, but during harvest season—late August and September in the Northern Hemisphere and six months opposite below the Equator—many brewers rush field-fresh hops to the brew kettle to create an ephemeral treat: wet-hopped beer.

"Wet hops" means that heat never zapped them from farm to bottle; "fresh hops" means that the brewery is using the freshest batch of dried hops, often within a week of processing. Don't expect palate ravagers, though. These IPAs taste graceful and subtle, focusing on fragrance rather than a bitter wallop. You'll commonly find these evanescent ales exclusively on tap at your local brewery or brewpub, but some producers are packaging them. The beers won't improve with a single passing day, however, so drink them as soon as you spot them. Now let's get wet.

★ ★ ★

HARVEST WET HOP IPA—NORTHERN HEMISPHERE

SIERRA NEVADA BREWING COMPANY | ABV: 6.7%
CHICO, CALIFORNIA | AVAILABLE: FALL
SIERRANEVADA.COM | GLASS: 🍺 | BITTERNESS: ★★☆☆

"If I'm making food and I go out to my garden and pull off fresh oregano for my pasta sauce, that's a wet hop," explains brewmaster Steve Dresler. "If I go to my spice cabinet and get the stuff I harvested earlier and dried, that's a baled hop. With wet hops, you're getting the hop at its maximum flavor and aroma potential." No brewery champions the flavorful potential of wet hops like Sierra Nevada. The Harvest collection features a quartet focusing on: a single hop, experimental hops, brewers' cut hops (samples sent to breweries for analysis and selection), and wet hops. Debuted in 1996, Northern Hemisphere put brewing ripe flowers straight from the fields on the map. Built from a simple base of two-row pale and caramel malts, it's scented and flavored with the lemon, grapefruit, and pine resin signature of Centennial and Cascade. The beers "should be purchased and consumed with a sense of urgency," Dresler says. "For me, the excitement is to find them as soon as you can and consume them as soon as you can."

Sierra Nevada retrofitted a device that extracts oil from mint plants to steam the hops, transforming the oils into vapor that they distill and use in their Hop Hunter IPA.

⏚ CHASIN' FRESHIES

DESCHUTES BREWERY | ABV: 7.4% (VARIES ANNUALLY)
BEND, OREGON | AVAILABLE: FALL
DESCHUTESBREWERY.COM | GLASS: 🍺 | BITTERNESS: ★★☆☆

Built on its Black Butte Porter and Obsidian Stout, Deschutes has matured into a polished IPA perfectionist. The citrusy Chainbreaker White IPA defines that category; Pinedrops tastes like its namesake tree; and Fresh Squeezed nails the juicy-tropical-citrusy trend. Come harvest, they embrace their proximity to hop fields and brew several farm-fresh beers, namely the herbal and citrusy Hop Trip Pale Ale and Chasin' Freshies, a delicious, oat-smoothed double entendre that nods to the pure powder of Mount Bachelor, the local ski slope, and the never-ending hunt for new hop varieties, including tropical Mosaic or citrusy Lemondrop. Results differ annually, but expect a bright, bitter, fragrant embodiment of fall's bounty.

Try your hand at harvesting Oregon hops by volunteering at Portland's Lucky Labrador Brewing Co., which throws a fall hop-picking party; then drink their fresh-hop Mutt IPA.

SARTORI HARVEST IPA

DRIFTWOOD BREWERY I ABV: 7%

VICTORIA, BRITISH COLUMBIA I AVAILABLE: FALL

DRIFTWOODBEER.COM I GLASS: 🍺 I BITTERNESS: ★★☆☆

As hop farms multiply worldwide, more brewers can make local wet-hopped beers. In B.C., Driftwood tackled the style first, in 2009. Brewmaster Jason Meyer combines Sartori Cedar Ranch's vibrant Centennial with hand-malted, locally grown barley to create this limited-edition, highly cultish brew, which regularly sells out within hours of its annual release. Orange-gold Sartori Harvest offers a rush of grass, orange peel, and grapefruit with a little bitterness and a dollop of malt sweetness to steady the ship. Also try Fat Tug, their year-round Northwest-style IPA.

🌾 HEAVY HANDED WET HOPPED IPA

TWO BROTHERS ARTISAN BREWING | ABV: 6.7%
WARRENVILLE, ILLINOIS | AVAILABLE: FALL
TWOBROTHERSBREWING.COM | GLASS: 🍺 | BITTERNESS: ★★☆☆

Siblings Jim and Jason Ebel began brewing to replicate the beers they loved while living in Europe. In
1996, they founded Two Brothers, which does well
with wheat beers, such as the banana-scented Ebel's
Weiss and spiced Monarch White, and IPAs, including the pine-forward Wobble and resinous Revelry Imperial Red. To champion the harvest, Two
Brothers builds a base IPA—amber, malt-forward,
sweet caramel—single-hopped with a trio of just-
harvested varietals: Centennial, Cascade, and Chinook. Pro tip: If you delight in doubles, try the
Heavier Handed IPA, 8.1% ABV and freighted
with Prairie State hops.

🌾 WARRIOR IPA

LEFT HAND BREWING COMPANY | ABV: 7.3%

LONGMONT, COLORADO | AVAILABLE: FALL

LEFTHANDBREWING.COM | GLASS: 🍺 | BITTERNESS: ★★☆☆

The hop industry has taken root quietly in Colorado, where the altitude, endless sunshine, and cool nights benefit growth. Each fall, Left Hand workers head to Rising Sun Farms to harvest ripe Cascade hops, bag 'em, and fly 'em back to Longmont, where brewers are cooking up this amber IPA. Matched with Centennial, the hops go straight into the kettles, lending a fresh, floral fragrance of pine resin and citrus that jibes with the biscuity, caramel malt character.

BREWERY SPOTLIGHT

4 PINES BREWING CO. | MANLY, AUSTRALIA 🇦🇺

To improve the subpar beer selection in this Sydney suburb, Jaron Mitchell founded 4 Pines (named for the removal of trees to install a machine gun battery during World War II) in 2008 as a brewpub pouring crisp kölsch and Citra-loaded pale ale. Having expanded into a new production facility, 4 Pines embraces experimentalism with its Keller Door series, doing imperial IPAs and all-organic, wet-hopped ales with equal aplomb.

DRINK: Fresh in Season IPA, made with the newest hops from the Northern and Southern Hemispheres.

꞊ GRAINS ꞊

When crafting IPA recipes, many brewers give their malt bill the green-screen treatment. The grains magically fade, allowing hops to perform CGI feats of flavor and aroma, but not every beer needs to aspire to *Crouching Hop Bine, Hidden Grain Bill*. Emphasis on grains can complement and give delicious new context to hop aromas and flavors. Used judiciously, rye can impart a dry, spicy complexity; wheat adds smoothness; and oats provide a silky luster.

WHEAT IPAS

As temperatures climb, banana-hinted German hefeweizens and delicately spiced Belgian witbiers colonize draft lines. The Venn-diagram overlap between them lies in their wheat. It imparts snowfall smoothness, foggy hue, and a touch of tartness. It also helps with head retention and enhancing aromatics. First popularized by the Lagunitas A Little Sumpin' Sumpin' Ale, the typically unfiltered hybrid has gone global. You'll find great examples in Alaska, where Midnight Sun makes the Hop Dog Double Wheat IPA, and Sweden's Beerbliotek, which doses each batch of its Wheat IPA with different hops. New Zealand's Renaissance makes its tangerine-pine White as Wheat IPA with native-grown American hops, including Cascade, Chinook, and Willamette. The wheat is on.

Look for the rise of the Oat IPA. New Belgium and Half Acre already collaborated on their Oatmeal IPA, and Arizona's Fate regularly releases tweaked versions of its Double Oatmeal IPA.

⚜ FORTUNATE ISLANDS

MODERN TIMES BEER | ABV: 5%

SAN DIEGO, CALIFORNIA | AVAILABLE: YEAR-ROUND

MODERNTIMESBEER.COM | GLASS: 🍺 | BITTERNESS: ★★☆☆

If its massive sticky-note collage of Michael Jackson and Bubbles the chimp doesn't make you fall in love with Modern Times, named for a failed Long Island utopia, nothing will. Their aroma-piloted, flavor-driven beers—

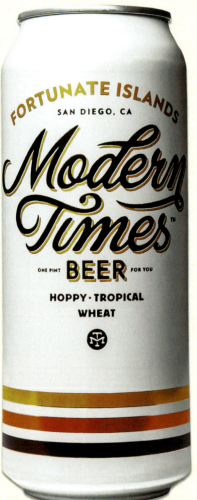

also named for bygone, collapsed Shangri-las—include the dank Blazing World Red IPA, rustic Lomaland Saison, and juicy-fruity City of the Sun IPA. For long-haul consumption, chart a course to Fortunate Islands, a fabled paradise supposedly settled by heroes from Greek mythology. The wheat beer–IPA hybrid stars 60 percent wheat and a touch of Caravienne malt, which gives the soft-sipper a subtle nuttiness (a hallmark of any utopia). Citra and Amarillo attend to the aromas of citrus, mangos, and passionfruit.

FUN FACT: Modern Times doubles as a coffee roaster, selling beans—sometimes barrel-aged—by the bag and infusing them into stouts, including the Black House.

🌾 A LITTLE SUMPIN' SUMPIN' ALE

LAGUNITAS BREWING COMPANY | ABV: 7.5%

PETALUMA, CALIFORNIA | AVAILABLE: YEAR-ROUND

LAGUNITAS.COM | GLASS: 🍺 | BITTERNESS: ★★☆☆

Made with 50 percent wheat and glutted with a pantryful of hops, including Centennial, Chinook, and spicy-herbal Santiam, Little is foggier than San Francisco Bay and comes bedecked with a chubby white head. It smells of citrus and spruce and drinks dang smooth, like a hefeweizen that set up camp in a hop field. It's a summer IPA for those who see no point in session beers—and in July you can find the even stronger Little Sumpin' Extra.

FUN FACT: Heineken purchased a half stake in Lagunitas (lah-goo-NEE-tuss) in 2015, which means this West Coast IPA is going global.

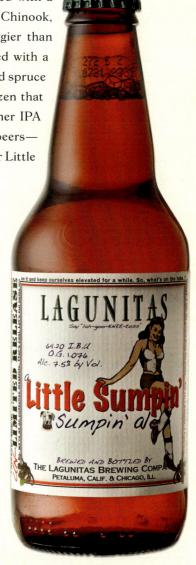

🌾 UPHEAVAL IPA

WIDMER BROTHERS BREWING I ABV: 7%

PORTLAND, OREGON I AVAILABLE: YEAR-ROUND

WIDMERBROTHERS.COM I GLASS: 🍺 I BITTERNESS: ★★★☆

Proclaiming a delicious beer a "wheat IPA" can misfire, though, as evidenced by Shock Top Wheat IPA's massive belly-flop. But name, shname: What you need to know is that unfiltered Upheaval has a grain bill with 40 percent wheat, which provides a smoggy hue and fuller body underpinning the catty, tropical profile showered with oranges and grapefruit. Two pounds of hops per barrel also pay dividends in the flavor department.

FUN FACT: Widmer Brothers released the gluten-reduced Omission IPA in 2013. Others quickly followed suit, including Canada's Glutenberg IPA.

🌾 VICIOUS AMERICAN WHEAT IPA

NORTH PEAK BREWING COMPANY I ABV: 6.7%

TRAVERSE CITY, MICHIGAN I AVAILABLE: YEAR-ROUND

NORTHPEAK.NET I GLASS: 🍺 I BITTERNESS: ★★☆☆

North Peak began in 1997 in the former Big Daylight Candy Factory. Today, the beer maker belongs to a collaborative clan that includes sour mavens Jolly Pumpkin. Ron Jeffries oversees their brewing operations, which knock out hop-centric beers such as the citrusy Wandered Session IPA and the Diabolical IPA, made with Michigan-grown Cascade and Chinook. Overcast and coppery, Vicious lands with intensity: Pine and citrus on the sniffer lead to earthy, herbal bitterness cut with crystal malt sweetness. If you want something imperial-strength, go for the Grizzly Peak releases, particularly the Humongous Midwest Red Ale.

FUN FACT: More and more hop fields are cropping up in Michigan, including Empire Hop Farms and Hop Head Farms.

🌾 80-ACRE HOPPY WHEAT BEER

BOULEVARD BREWING CO. | ABV: 5.5%

KANSAS CITY, MISSOURI | AVAILABLE: YEAR-ROUND

BOULEVARD.COM | GLASS: 🍺 | BITTERNESS: ★☆☆☆

Boulevard has been keen on wheat since its 1989 beginning. Evidence: its linchpin brew, the cloudy, quenching Unfiltered Wheat Beer. They also go against the grain with their fruity, peppery Tank 7 Farmhouse Ale, sprightly Ginger Lemon Radler, and an array of IPAs: grapefruit-spritzed Single-Wide; lavishly hopped, tropical double Calling; and 80-Acre Hoppy Wheat Beer. Sip this low-ABV mixture of past and future that balloons with oranges and grass, fluffy and refreshing with scant bitterness.

BREWERY SPOTLIGHT

GREAT LEAP BREWING | BEIJING, CHINA 🇨🇳

To remedy the homogeneity of Chinese lager, Ohio native Carl Setzer, then working at a Beijing tech firm, and friend Dane Vanden Berg founded Great Leap, which brews with indigenous ingredients, from the roasted malts fueling Pale Ale #6 to the Honey Ma Gold Ale tingling with floral Sichuan peppercorns. The brewery's General collection of IPAs includes rye, black, and the session-strength Hidden General, flavored with oolong tea and chrysanthemum flowers.

DRINK: Ghost General Wheat IPA, made with native Qingdao flower hops.

RYE IPAS

Rye whiskey—dry, spicy, peppery, invigorating—lacks the corn sweetness of bourbon. It's prickly, rough-edged, crammed with character, and perfect for sipping on a Saturday night. Following in the footsteps of their distiller brethren, brewers have tapped this grain for their handiwork, creating IPAs with sharpened contours, spiciness either subtle or overt, and a drought-dry finish. Try Sierra Nevada Ruthless Rye, Founders Red's IPA, or Blue Point Rastafa Rye for a perfect primer on the grain's power. Rye also has its drawbacks, however. It can create a sticky, viscous mash, so it does its best work in smaller quantities, like a scene-stealing supporting player. Here are five worth your time.

HABITUS RYE IPA

MIKE HESS BREWING OF SAN DIEGO | ABV: 8%

SAN DIEGO, CALIFORNIA | AVAILABLE: YEAR-ROUND

MIKEHESSBREWING.COM | GLASS: 🍺🍷 | BITTERNESS: ★★★☆

Since 2010, this nanobrewery—Hess's hobby relocated into an 800-square-foot garage—has gone supernova into one of Southern California's brightest stars. Burnishing its rep are Grazias, a smooth and nutty Vienna cream ale; refreshing Claritas Kölsch; and Solis Occasus ("sunset" in Latin), an evolving collection of dry, San Diego–style IPAs. Despite its strength, Habitus, which won gold at the 2014 World Beer Cup, remains perilously, perfectly drinkable. The characteristic earth and spice give way to the herbal, pine-scented verve of indulgent hopping with Chinook and Sterling.

FUN FACT: Mike Hess was San Diego's first brewery to acquire a canning line.

RHYE IPA

SMUTTYNOSE BREWING COMPANY | ABV: 7.7%

HAMPTON, NEW HAMPSHIRE | AVAILABLE: LATE WINTER

SMUTTYNOSE.COM | GLASS: 🍺 | BITTERNESS: ★★☆☆

The Smuttynose portfolio includes a goodly selection of IPAs, especially the citrus-focused Finestkind, hulking Big A Double IPA, and Rhye. Formerly part of their Big Beer series—a collection of toothsome weirdos such as the Rocky Road Dessert Stout and Frankenlager, an India pale lager—the richly golden Rhye IPA was so good that it became a cold-weather seasonal, testament to its mélange of rye spice and modern hops, including papaya-like Citra and Falconer's Flight, run through with grapefruit, lemon, and a charge of bitterness. Oh, and Albrecht Dürer, the famous sixteenth-century German artist, drew the label's Indian rhinoceros.

FUN FACT: Smuttynose's Smuttlabs division specializes in oddball, experimental beers, such as the Smoked Peach Short Weisse and Granite State Destroyer, an "imperial corn lager."

🌾 HOP ROD RYE

BEAR REPUBLIC BREWING CO. | ABV: 8%

HEALDSBURG, CALIFORNIA | AVAILABLE: YEAR-ROUND

BEARREPUBLIC.COM | GLASS: 🍺 | BITTERNESS: ★★☆☆

For almost two decades, Bear Republic has stood as one of America's best IPA breweries, led by the golden, floral Racer 5 IPA and other members of the hop-intensive Racer pack. (Chase down the piney, citrusy Café Racer 15 and soundly malt-orange Racer X.) They also love rye-loading a brew kettle, turning out the Belgian-style Ryevalry Double IPA, which won gold at the 2010 Great American Beer Festival, and the high-test Hop Rod Rye. Brewed with 18 percent rye, this aromatic amber IPA makes for a sticky sipper, revved with caramel goodness and malt-cutting spicy pepper. Conclusion: dry, bitter, and enduring.

FUN FACT: Bear Republic supplies its Racer 5 IPA to California distillery Charbay, which double-distills it and ages it in French oak, creating the R5 Hop-Flavored Whiskey.

🌾 RYE IPA

LERVIG AKTIEBRYGGERI | ABV: 8.5%

STAVANGER, NORWAY | AVAILABLE: YEAR-ROUND

LERVIG.NO | GLASS: 🍷 | BITTERNESS: ★★★☆

In 2003, the beer drinkers of this port town were displeased. Carlsberg shuttered the local brewery responsible for making Ringnes lager. In response, locals started Lervig, a cooperative that initially produced light lagers that left much to be desired. In 2010, American expat Mike Murphy, a brewing savant, mapped a flavorful new path for Lervig with U.S.-inspired beers such as the tropical, grapefruit-scented Lucky Jack Pale Ale and brawny, oatmeal-driven Konrad's Stout. Their strong, nicely spicy, generously bittered Rye IPA pairs pine, resin, and citrus rind with bready caramel sweetness for equilibrium.

🌾 WYTCHMAKER RYE IPA

JESTER KING BREWERY | ABV: 6%

AUSTIN, TEXAS | AVAILABLE: ROTATING

JESTERKINGBREWERY.COM | GLASS: 🍷 | BITTERNESS: ★★☆☆

If you've studied the Salem Witch Trials in depth, you may know that ergot, a fungus from which LSD derives, infected a local rye crop at the time. Nodding to that trippy kernel of history, this farmhouse brewery conjured an IPA heavy on organic rye and rice hulls—which keep grains from sticking during brewing—plus wild yeast and souring bacteria harvested from the surrounding Hill Country. Add some aroma-centric hops (Citra, Simcoe, Cascade), and you have an engagingly tart and funky take on the rye IPA, earthy and plucky with pepper, citrus, and tropical fruit.

BREWERY SPOTLIGHT

EDGE BREWING | BARCELONA, SPAIN 🇪🇸

American expats Scott Vanover and Alan Sheppard import everything: overnighting yeast from the States, cold-shipping hops, and brewing U.S.-style beers, such as the California-worthy Hoptimista IPA; Eternal Sunshine, made with orange peel, juice, and zest; and Cookie Euphoria Amber Ale.

DRINK: Taronja HoRyezon Rye IPA, first brewed with Florida's Due South and which contains local honey and Valencia oranges.

⹁ COLORS ⹁

If you teleported back to 1994, your standard beer choices would consist of blonde, brown, and red ales and black stouts and porters. Color often correlated to flavor, a concept as easy to grasp as, well, a cold pint glass. Beer today ain't so plain-Jane. Brewers go all-terrain with wild yeast; unconventional grains, such as spelt; and spices worthy of a Michelin-starred kitchen. Brewing has flown far from those cut-and-dried days of color, but, as always, it's boomeranging back. These red, white, and black hues sometimes provide little clue to the flavors that await, though, so let's color your understanding of what's what.

RED IPAS

The red IPA relates closely to the East Coast IPA of yore, darker and sweeter than today's incarnation. The source: healthy doses of caramel or crystal malt for the arterial tint, sweetness, and flavors that evoke raisins or toffee. Making these malts first requires stewing, which creates crystalline structures that caramelize when kilned and also darken the brew. Since yeast can't convert cooked sugars, the grains enhance foam and add color and sweetness. In other words, today's breweries use a red IPA's sweetness to foil bitterness and complement hops redolent of berries, citrus, and pine. Picture a sugar-sprinkled bowl of strawberries and grapefruit, and drink these reds ASAP. As the beer ages, the crystal malts develop notes of dried fruit or raisins that overwhelm the fast-receding hop aromas and flavors.

🌾 NUGGET NECTAR

TRÖEGS INDEPENDENT BREWING | ABV: 7.5%
HERSHEY, PENNSYLVANIA | AVAILABLE: WINTER
TROEGS.COM | GLASS: 🍺 | BITTERNESS: ★★★☆

Right when winter turns your mood darker than frozen street slush, Tröegs releases the morale-boosting Nugget Nectar, a harbinger of better days. It may seem odd that this amplified version of their Hopback Amber Ale arrives during subzero season, but remember: Farmers harvest hops in late summer. Months pass before the flowers are processed and distributed to brewers, meaning the freshest hop-laced beers can double as holiday presents. Bright orange Nugget Nectar teems with Simcoe, Warrior, and (of course) Nugget hops, then circulates through a hopback machine stuffed with even *more* Nugget hops, infusing the beer with a penetratingly fresh herbal, grassy aroma in lockstep with flavors of caramel and pine—just the jolt needed to escape those seasonal doldrums. For the next cold snap, also try the citrusy, fruity Blizzard of Hops.

"Come November and December, we start getting hops in from the fall harvest, and of course we want to brew something really hoppy right away. Back in 2004, we were looking to do something with Nugget hops. We'd been kicking around the name Nugget Nectar, too. . . . That first year it came out, right around John's birthday, we hit upon this perfect storm of a great beer with a great name at the right time of year."

—Chris Trogner, cofounder,
Tröegs Independent Brewing

🌾 TOASTER PASTRY

21ST AMENDMENT | ABV: 7.6%

SAN LEANDRO, CALIFORNIA | AVAILABLE: YEAR-ROUND

21ST-AMENDMENT.COM | GLASS: 🍺 | BITTERNESS: ★★☆☆

Innovation is one thing, but gimmicky stunt beers rub me the wrong way. When 21st Amendment, a San Francisco area brewpub that long contract-brewed IPAs such as Brew Free! or Die and Back in Black in Minnesota, opened a brewery in a former Kellogg's factory, news of this commemorative beer—a red IPA modeled on Pop-Tarts—struck a cynical nerve. A single taste, however, and all skepticism popped like a beer bubble. This crimson ale nails that soft, bready flavor, ably evoking strawberry jam with a mixture of pale and dark crystal malts. Calypso powers the fruity aroma and provides just enough bitterness to prevent sugar shock. The best part: Toaster Pastry comes in 19.2-ounce cans, meaning there's more beer to love. Lesson? Keep an open mind *and* an open mouth.

FUN FACT: Cofounder Shaun O'Sullivan's nickname is El Sully, immortalized in the name of the brewery's Mexican-style lager.

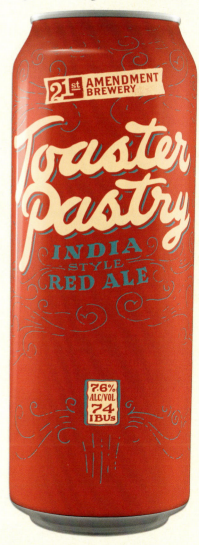

🌾 MISSISSIPPI FIRE ANT

SOUTHERN PROHIBITION BREWING | ABV: 8%
HATTIESBURG, MISSISSIPPI | AVAILABLE: YEAR-ROUND
SOPROBREWING.COM | GLASS: 🍺 | BITTERNESS: ★★☆☆

Founded in 2013 in a former furniture showroom, SoPro follows a two-pronged mission to "brew great beer and help make Mississippi a great place to live." The beer scene here is still young, so they play it safe with accessible

blonde ales and ESBs, complemented by daring Cicada Series seasonals, including Pow! Rye in the Kisser, a spring-friendly rye ale brightened with Lemondrop hops; fall's Sinister Minister Black IPA, which medalled gold at the 2014 World Beer Championship; and an annually shifting IPA, unveiled in early summer. A strong and rich red ale crammed with flavors of toffee and caramel, Mississippi Fire Ant tastes lightly spicy and finely fruity, and the escalated alcohol never bites too hard.

FUN FACT: Mississippi legalized homebrewing only in 2013.

♦ HORIZON RED IPA

SUMMIT BREWING COMPANY | ABV: 5.7%

ST. PAUL, MINNESOTA | AVAILABLE: YEAR-ROUND

SUMMITBREWING.COM | GLASS: 🍺 | BITTERNESS: ★★☆☆

Instead of getting a master's in social work, Mark Stutrud turned an auto-parts warehouse into Summit, named for the capital's stately avenue, in 1986. The Extra Pale Ale—a biscuity, fragrant beauty and one of the first brews he produced—remains an Upper Midwest stalwart. Summit's IPAs encompass fruity, earthy True Brit and Sága, suffused with tropical Citra and New Zealand's peachy and apricot-like

Rakau hops. This IPA takes its name not from a Cold War spy novel but from Horizon hops, a spicy, floral cultivar developed in 1970. Suffused with chameleonic Mosaic and floral Cascade and an amalgam of German, American, and English malts, Horizon Red punches above its ABV and tastes smooth and sweetly malty, dankly seasoned with citrus and pine.

ᘒ TALL POPPY

8 WIRED BREWING CO. | ABV: 7%

WARKWORTH, NEW ZEALAND | AVAILABLE: YEAR-ROUND

8WIRED.CO.NZ | GLASS: 🍺 | BITTERNESS: ★★☆☆

After five years of contract-brewing across New Zealand, 8 Wired—the gauge for sheep fencing that Kiwis used for DIY fixes—operates this production brewery north of Auckland. Founder Søren Eriksen hammers out "new world interpretations of old world styles," which boils down to goosing the hop load. For example, he barrel-ages a saison with wild yeast, then dry-hops it with Kohatu and Motueka. The imperial-strength, sturdily bitter iStout abounds with herbal Chinook and citrusy Cascade. An "India red ale," the ruby-toned Tall Poppy teems with three kinds of crystal malt, creating a caramel spine and hops both fruity (hello, Amarillo) and bracingly bitter.

FUN FACT: Eriksen began brewing after his future wife, Monique, gave him a homebrew kit as a Christmas present.

BREWERY SPOTLIGHT

LIBERTY BREWING CO. | AUCKLAND, NEW ZEALAND

After taking over Liberty Supplies, an online homebrew shop, Joseph and Christina Wood settled on a unique sales tactic: Brew beer with the ingredients and offer prospective customers a taste. The offerings—Yakima Monster Pale Ale, C!tra Imperial IPA, and Knife Party IPA—feature bear hugs of hops and proved so popular that they shuttered the homebrew business and expanded the brewery.

DRINK: Yakima Scarlet, a red ale hopped with Warrior, Centennial, Cascade, and Columbus.

MODUS OPERANDI | MONA VALE, AUSTRALIA

Husband and wife Grant and Jaz Wearin spent six months motorhoming across America, exploring the brewing landscape and returning to Australia with a stupendous souvenir: D. J. McCready, former Oskar Blues brewer, as head brewer at Modus Operandi. His handiwork includes Zoo Feeder IPA, bitten with citrus and pine; Centennial-crammed M.O.na Pale; and refreshing Kite Flyer Cream Ale.

DRINK: Former Tenant Red IPA, tropically scented with Galaxy and Mosaic.

WHITE IPAS

Wheat and white IPAs may seem interchangeable, two sides of the same cloudy coin. Both rely heavily on wheat, but a world of difference exists between them. The white IPA descends from the lightly spicy, unfiltered Belgian witbier. Brewers no longer commercially produced witbiers by 1960, so Belgian milkman Pierre Celis homebrewed a batch and, encouraged by the response, opened a brewery in the former stables abutting his house. He called it Oud Hoegaards Bier, better known as Hoegaarden, and revived the style from extinction. This wheat-steered, delicate farmhouse ale classically flavored with coriander and orange peel represents one of brewing's finest please-everyone styles, buoyed by the breakneck success (and advertising largesse) of Blue Moon as well as the independent Allagash White.

A new generation toed up to the witbier's citrus to springboard the "white beer" into the realm of the India pale. Some versions hew close to the source, such as Deschutes Chainbreaker, an early example that cranks up the citrus with Cascade and Centennial. Others go crazy with spicing, including the Upslope Thai Style White IPA, which uses basil and lemongrass to evoke Southeast Asia.

Words to the wise: Don't expect a label to tell you the entire tale. Some so-called white IPAs lack any spice—looking at you, New Belgium Accumulation and Hopworks Pig War—but you should spice up your life with this eclectic quartet.

☙ FRESH SLICE

OTTER CREEK BREWING COMPANY | ABV: 5.5%
MIDDLEBURY, VERMONT | AVAILABLE: SPRING
OTTERCREEKBREWING.COM | GLASS: 🍺 | BITTERNESS: ★★☆☆

Founded in 1991, Otter Creek drew drinkers' love for its altbier-style Cop-
per Ale and Stovepipe Porter, euro-influenced beers that washed across
1990s New England. Today's trends run smoother and more hop-socked, so
the Vermonters ditched the dated beers and branding, replacing them with
highly perfumed, seriously hopped libations, such as the juicy Backseat Ber-
ner IPA and the orangey Over Easy IPA, packaged with counterculture cartoon labels featuring brewmaster Mike Gerhart. Super-unfiltered, fogged-up
Fresh Slice pulls its flavor from coriander, clementine juice, and orange peel,
a citrus rush tailored for summertime thirst-quenching. Also pay attention
to the Belgian yeast's zesty contribution.

🌾 GALAXY WHITE IPA

ANCHORAGE BREWING COMPANY | ABV: 7%

ANCHORAGE, ALASKA | AVAILABLE: ROTATING

ANCHORAGEBREWINGCOMPANY.COM | GLASS: 🍷 | BITTERNESS: ★★☆☆

Gabe Fletcher has no plans to conquer the brewing world, nor does he ache to re-create brews from 1798. At ABC, he focuses on barrel-fermentation in concert with souring bacteria and wild yeast. His au courant creations include the triple-fermented Belgian-style Bitter Monk Double IPA and the Tides and Its Takers tripel, a Dogfish Head collaboration that deploys lemony Sorachi Ace. The sublimely fruity, funky, spicy Galaxy pays tribute to path-carving exploration, spiced with black peppercorns, kumquats, coriander, and (of course) gobs of Galaxy hops.

FUN FACT: Anchorage Brewing's Culmination Festival gathers some of the globe's choicest, most cultish brewers. Past participants have included the Alchemist, Cellarmaker, and Hill Farmstead.

🌾 NOT JUST ANOTHER WIT

MIKKELLER | ABV: 7.6%

COPENHAGEN, DENMARK | AVAILABLE: ROTATING

MIKKELLER.DK | GLASS: 🍺 | BITTERNESS: ★★☆☆

In the late Aughts, Belgian-style witbiers, lifted by Blue Moon, appeared everywhere, every one cloudy and seasoned with the unwavering duo of coriander and orange peel. To subvert the status quo, Mikkel Borg Bjergsø, teacher-turned-prolific-globetrotting-gypsy brewer, revved up the booze and hops, relying on standard IPA cultivars, such as Amarillo and Cascade. Capped with a huge head, this creamy beer tastes indubitably floral and citrusy, but it has echoes of pine and pineapples, and a dry, herbal bitterness rolls across your palate. Buy it by the bottle, or sample it at one of Mikkeller Bar's international outposts (Bangkok, Barcelona, Reykjavik, Seoul, Tokyo, and counting).

FUN FACT: Mikkel Borg Bjergsø's twin brother is Jeppe Jarnit-Bjergsø, the brains behind Evil Twin (page 171).

❦ THAI STYLE WHITE IPA

UPSLOPE BREWING COMPANY | ABV: 6.5%
BOULDER, COLORADO | AVAILABLE: LATE SUMMER / FALL
UPSLOPEBREWING.COM | GLASS: 🍺 | BITTERNESS: ★☆☆☆

For the 2012 Great American Beer Festival, Ryan Conklin had a notion: Wouldn't a beer that mimicked Thai curry taste grand? The beer director at Denver's Euclid Hall, one of America's top brew-focused restaurants, approached Upslope with the inkling that became Thai Style White IPA, spiced with cinnamon, Thai basil, lemongrass, and ginger. The brew proved so popular that Upslope—known for canned beers such as the dry and spicy Pale Ale and piney, floral Imperial India Pale Ale—refined the recipe, turning it into a late-summer standby. Paved with wheat and witbier yeast, the smooth IPA features Galaxy and Cascade, which impart a citrusy, tropical pleasure suited for the heat of a green curry in August.

BLACK IPAS

A *dark* pale ale? What? This most contentious, maligned, and renamed of all IPA variants also goes by India black ale, India dark ale, dark IPA, and Cascadian dark ale, a geographic nod to where the style originated. Further obfuscating matters, the style-setting Beer Judge Certification Program calls it American black ale.

Agree to disagree on the name if you like, but recognize that this sludge-colored brew does have defining characteristics. It boasts generous amounts of hops—harking back to England's dark, well-bittered porters of yore—which makes it as assertively scented as its lighter brethren. However, two brewing workarounds leave the roasty astringency at a low level. First, brewers can steep the dark malts in cold water, drawing out flavor and color but not harshness. (Think of cold-brew coffee, chocolaty, low in acidity, and so easy to drink.) They also use dehusked or debittered malt that achieves the same end. These techniques create dark beers that drink light and dry, as fragrant as a field and barely bitter, the roast dancing calmly with hops. So let's take a drink on the dark side.

🌾 WOOKEY JACK

FIRESTONE WALKER BREWING COMPANY | ABV: 8.3%

PASO ROBLES, CALIFORNIA | AVAILABLE: YEAR-ROUND

FIRESTONEBEER.COM | GLASS: 🍺🍷 | BITTERNESS: ★★★☆

America's most decorated brewer glides beneath the beer-geek radar. The Great American Beer Festival has named Matt Brynildson—bushy-goateed brewmaster now at Firestone—Brewer of the Year *four* times, and the World Beer Cup has crowned him champion brewmaster the same number of times. While still at SLO Brewing, he won the inaugural gold for an American-style India pale ale at the 2000 GABF. His trophy chest swells with medals for the English-inspired DBA Pale Ale, citrusy Pale 31, hoppy Pivo Pilsner, Double Jack Imperial IPA, and Velvet Merlin Oatmeal Stout. To that list, add roasty Wookey Jack, an unfiltered black IPA made spicy with several kinds of rye and fruity with tropical-citrus Citra and Amarillo dry-hopping.

FUN FACT: To keep light from skunking Firestone's beers, Brynildson instituted an ironclad rule: no daytime dry-hopping. The brewery now uses closed hop cannons, but that zealous attention to detail earned him a lasting nickname, he says. "All of my close brewer friends still call me Batman because of it."

🌾 BLACK BETTY

BEAVERTOWN BREWERY | ABV: 7.4%

LONDON, ENGLAND | AVAILABLE: YEAR-ROUND

BEAVERTOWNBREWERY.CO.UK | GLASS: 🍺 | BITTERNESS: ★★☆☆

Logan Plant caught the brewing bug after a post-concert boozing session at Brooklyn's Fette Sau. Back in London, the singer decided to start Duke's Brew & Que in De Beauvoir Town (aka Beavertown). Steered by head brewer Jenn Merrick, named 2015 brewer of the year by the British Guild of Beer Writers, Beavertown kills it with hop-forward, American-inspired formulations, including the juicy, tropical Gamma Ray Pale Ale; orange zest–laced Bloody 'Ell IPA; and 8 Ball Rye IPA. Wheat smooths their Black Betty, a dark jewel light on bitterness and roast, while Chinook and Citra heap on aromatics of Caribbean fruit, Florida citrus, and Oregon pine.

FUN FACT: Logan is the youngest son of Led Zeppelin's Robert Plant.

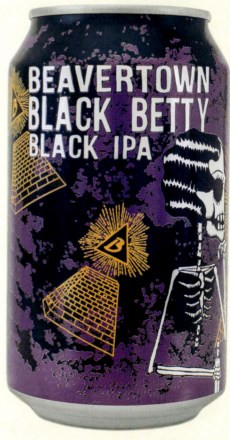

☆ B SPACE INVADER

BIRRIFICIO TOCCALMATTO | ABV: 6.3%

FIDENZA, ITALY | AVAILABLE: YEAR-ROUND

BIRRATOCCALMATTO.COM | GLASS: 🍺 | BITTERNESS: ★★☆☆

Too often, black IPAs become dumpster fires of roast and bitterness that you wouldn't wish on your enemies. Nailing the balance between dark and dank, or light char and citrus, presents a huge struggle. Happily, Toccalmatto can reaffirm your faith in the sub-category with, in their words, an "intergalactic black Cascadian incredible pale ale." Crystal malt and chocolate wheat build a taste platform of coffee and toffee, cocoa and licorice. Galaxy—as well as other cultivars, including Amarillo and Simcoe—fuels the stellar aroma of citrus, peaches, and pine. The result: otherworldly.

FUN FACT: The name of the brewery translates to "a touch of madness." Prior to founding Toccalmatto, Bruno Carilli worked for Carlsberg.

🌾 DARK HOPS

BEER HERE | ABV: 8.5%

KØBENHAVN, DENMARK | AVAILABLE: YEAR-ROUND

BEERHERE.DK | GLASS: 🍷 | BITTERNESS: ★★☆☆

"Do not waste your thirst" goes the slogan steering this gypsy brewery piloted by legendary Danish brewer Christian Skovdal Andersen. The summery, Citra-crowded Wicked Wheat, West Coast–inspired Executioner IPA, or floral and spicy Hopfix Rye IPA—none of his beers plays the shrinking violet. Dark Hops answers an easy question: What happens when a burly stout hops into bed with a bitter IPA? They create this inky warmer layered with flavors of roasted coffee, bittersweet chocolate, and a nice citrus squeeze. Almost no IPAs benefit from aging, but this specimen, brash and intense when fresh, makes a good case for cellaring. Age brings mellowness, moving it in line with a porter.

FUN FACT: Andersen draws all his own labels.

BREWERY SPOTLIGHT

CERVECERIA INSURGENTE | TIJUANA

"We are a group of rebels dedicated to liberating you from the tyranny of flavorless beer," says Insurgente, which brothers Ivan and Damian Morales founded on the balcony of their mother's apartment. Living in Los Angeles helped Ivan refine his taste for better beer, expressed today with Belgian-style witbier Tiniebla; La Lupulosa ("the Hoppy One"), a West Coast–style IPA with a blend of five different hops; and the wet-hopped Lupulillo Rivera Pale Ale.

DRINK: Nocturna, chocolatey and roasty, Mexico's first commercially bottled black IPA.

No longer the land of just Corona, Pacifico, and Tecate, Mexico's beer scene is evolving rapidly, especially in Baja and sprawling metropolises, such as Mexico City and Guadalajara. The industry opened wider in 2013 thanks to the efforts of Minerva Brewing, which helped advance legislation that limited the country's two big brewers—Grupo Modelo and Cuauhtemoc-Moctezuma, which control more than 95 percent of the market—from quashing competition with exclusivity contracts at bars, restaurants, and stores.

BROWN OUT

Eyeball the IPA color wheel and you'll notice one missing from most shelves: brown. Early on, Dogfish Head demonstrated that darker IPAs had commercial legs. The 1999 Indian Brown Ale amalgamated a Scotch ale, IPA, and American-style brown ale, but that brew didn't plant a flag in a style. (In 2016, Dogfish Head relabeled India Brown as a "dark India pale ale.) Nor did Terrapin, which made their India Style Brown Ale (renamed Hop Karma and retired). Avery created a one-off anniversary beer dubbed an "imperial India-style brown ale," and for a brief spell Boulder Beer made their Flashback India-style brown ale year-round. That nomenclature still exists, but more concise terms—"brown IPA" and "hoppy brown ale"—are replacing it slowly.

The style expectedly conjoins a brown ale and an IPA, grounded with chocolate and toffee, maybe biscuits and caramel, and malt-powered, minus the overbearing sweetness. The hops sing floral, fruity, or piney, and the bitterness bites robustly but not to extremes. For good examples, try the Epic Santa Cruz Brown IPA, SweetWater Hash Brown, and Smuttynose Durty, a double IPA wrapped around a caramel nugget.

Malt-centered IPAs of all tones make for a tougher sell, and unfortunately the black IPA tends to overshadow this lighter shade of pale. Brown IPAs aren't disappearing, though, so next time you find yourself in a beer store, see what brown can do for you.

⇒ YEAST-DRIVEN ⇐

Brewers might as well be dumpster diving if they don't have healthy, happy yeast. That's how important our little microbial friends are to ensuring that wort becomes flavorful, engaging beer instead of bitter grain water.

With IPAs, many breweries opt for clean-fermenting, lightly fruity yeast strains, such as White Labs' California Ale Yeast or Wyeast Laboratories' American Ale, both rumored to come from Sierra Nevada Pale Ale. Hops won't relinquish the catbird seat, but brewers are tapping the characteristics of yeast strains, using them to drive flavor. They're fermenting IPAs with fruity, clove-like Belgian yeast, lager strains (hello, IPL!), and *Brettanomyces*, which conjures tropical flavors in line with today's top hops.

INDIA PALE LAGERS

However prevalent, India pale ales hardly count as the world's most popular beer style. That distinction goes to the bubbly, crisp, crowd-pleasing, innocuous, ubiquitous lager. When craft brewers started battling Big Beer in the early 1980s, they took first aim at a radioactive ocean of bland lagers and pilsners. To compete against the giants, they needed flavor rather than marketing slogans. As the global beer scene has matured, craft breweries have begun returning to lagers, and for good reason.

Lagern means "to rest" in German, and a lengthy fermentation gives lagers their trademark brisk refreshment. Instead of fresh spins on, say, a "triple-hopped" Miller Lite (ahem), brewers are imbuing lagers with gobs of hops, often enough to rival the most perfumed IPAs. This style-straddler has taken the name India pale lager—IPL, if brevity's your bag.

Ale yeasts typically throw off fruit notes, which can mask hops' singular flavors and aromas, but with lager yeast brewers can construct a clean platform that allows hops to take center stage and deliver a trumpet blast of olfactory pleasure.

HOPONIUS UNION

JACK'S ABBY | ABV: 6.7%

FRAMINGHAM, MASSACHUSETTS | AVAILABLE: YEAR-ROUND

JACKSABBY.COM | GLASS: 🍺 | BITTERNESS: ★★☆☆

Craft brewers long gave cool fermentation the cold shoulder, brewing anything and everything but lagers. Where some brewers saw a scapegrace, brothers Eric, Sam, and Jack Hendler saw opportunity. In 2011, they founded Jack's Abby (named for Jack's wife), specializing in tradition-flouting, bottom-fermented beers glutted with hops, spices, and souring bacteria. Their category-redefining creations include a tart Berliner-style lager, witbier-inspired Leisure Time, and Mass Rising, a double IPA with lager DNA. You'll have a hard time passing up the crisp, fruity Hoponius Union, a citrusy, tropical reimagining of the West Coast IPA.

🌾 IHL

CAMDEN TOWN BREWERY | ABV: 6.2%

LONDON, ENGLAND | AVAILABLE: YEAR-ROUND

CAMDENTOWNBREWERY.COM | GLASS: 🍺 | BITTERNESS: ★★☆☆

Jaspar Cuppidge's grandmother ran an Australian brewery, and he started brewing in the basement of his pub, the Horseshoe, because he found most commercially available lagers bland or expensive. Located beneath a railway arch in the London district of the same name, Camden Town specializes in lagers: piney, unfiltered Pils, inky Black Friday Pilsner, and clean and quenching Camden Hells Lager, its flagship take on a Munich helles. The ABV-boosted India Helles Lager (IHL) brims with American Simcoe, Chinook, and Mosaic. Lightly foggy and richly golden, it hits with grapefruit and ripe peaches, but its crisp snap and fine effervescence keep it fragrantly refreshing.

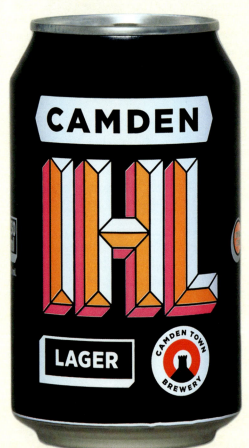

FUN FACT: AB InBev bought Camden Town in 2015.

🌾 IN-TENTS IPL

BASE CAMP BREWING COMPANY | ABV: 6.8%

PORTLAND, OREGON | AVAILABLE: YEAR-ROUND

BASECAMPBREWINGCO.COM | GLASS: 🍺 | BITTERNESS: ★★☆☆

In lieu of a bill-paying IPA, Base Camp pounds a different path to profitability. The brewery takes recipe inspiration from nature and outdoor activities, creating both the expected, such as the S'more Stout, and unexpected, including the Salmonberry River Dunkel, an earthy, pine-hit, cedar-licked exploration of terroir tinged with Oregon sea salt. In-Tents, their invigorating, copper-colored, flagship IPL, offers all the floral, pine-focused aromas you associate with the Pacific Northwest, but toasty malt and an understated woody note, courtesy of aging on red and white oak, complement the fragrance. Grab it by the can or this 22-ounce aluminum bottle.

BREWERY SPOTLIGHT

BIRRA DEL BORGO | BORGOROSE, ITALY 🇮🇹

Northwest of Rome, Leonardo di Vincenzo, a biochemist-turned-brewer, makes oyster stouts, gentian root–seasoned ales, and strong hybrids starring grape must—but let's talk hops: His amber ReAle updates the historic IPA template with citrus-forward American flowers, magnified in the embiggened Extra.

DRINK: My Antonia, originally made with Dogfish Head, an amplified pilsner mixing Saaz with Simcoe and Warrior.

SIGTUNA BRYGGHUS | ARLANDASTAD, SWEDEN 🇸🇪

Founded in 2006, this low-key brewery northeast of Stockholm began with a mead, altbier, and golden ale. No longer small potatoes, they now produce organic IPAs in single and double strength, a hefeweizen heaped with tropical American hops, and style-busters galore.

DRINK: East River Lager, freighted with Cascade and Hallertauer.

BELGIAN IPAS

Belgium might seem like the promised land of monk-made elixirs, rustic farmhouse ales, and beers conjured spontaneously from thin air, but the kingdom loves its lager (mainly the forgettable Jupiler). Nor have Belgian brewers shied away from hops. A single taste of Saison Dupont will put paid to that notion.

Both European and American brewers honor the Belgian IPA by using Belgian yeast. That means the spice is right, cloves and fruitiness often are present, hops abound, and so on. The Belgian IPA, like a magpie, snatches bits and bobs of American, English, and European ingenuity and fashions it into a compelling new quaff with too many angles to fit neatly into a box. The American Belgian IPA uses the same yeast strain but ups the bitter, aromatic ante with American hops. Try the Flying Dog Raging Bitch or Stone's Cali-Belgique IPA, and you'll understand the joys of punching your drinking passport with these border-blurring IPAs.

🌾 HUGH MALONE ALE

ALLAGASH BREWING COMPANY | ABV: VARIES
PORTLAND, MAINE | AVAILABLE: ROTATING
ALLAGASH.COM | GLASS: 🍺🍷| BITTERNESS: ★★☆☆

Hugh Malone—sounds like a salty old local, right? Nope. It's a pun on humulone, a bitter compound lurking in hop resin. (For Allagash's extended take on the joke, head to hughmalone.com.) You probably know Allagash for their spiced White, spontaneously fermented Coolship series, and Curieux, a bourbon barrel–aged tripel, but Hugh is their annual mash-up of American and Belgian brewing styles. Altered annually, good old Hugh remains finely fruity with a fat white head. A fragrant goulash of cutting-edge hops, including Azacca and Galaxy, supply the aromatics.

FUN FACT: A buck from every four-pack goes to support community gardens, so drink up and do good.

🌾 XX BITTER

BROUWERIJ DE RANKE | ABV: 6%

WEVELGEM, BELGIUM | AVAILABLE: YEAR-ROUND

DERANKE.BE | GLASS: 🍺 BITTERNESS: ★★★☆

When buddies Nino Bacelle and Guido Devos
devised this unfiltered, unpasteurized ale, they
aimed for aggression, wanting to brew "the hoppi-
est beer of Belgium," as the early labels boasted.
They started with a clean base of pilsner malt and
a truckload of spicy, herbal Hallertau and sharply
bitter Brewer's Gold hops. XX is no brute, though.
It drinks dry, with helter-skelter carbonation,
and an enduring earthy bitterness. For a bigger
aromatic hit, grab the XXX Bitter, made with
50 percent more hops.

🌾 POPERINGS HOMMEL

BROUWERIJ VAN EECKE | ABV: 7.5%

WATOU, BELGIUM | AVAILABLE: YEAR-ROUND

BROUWERIJVANEECKE.BE | GLASS: 🍷 | BITTERNESS: ★★☆☆

During World War I, catastrophe befell West Flanders. Bombs destroyed the grain and hop fields. After the armistice, locals rebuilt and replanted hops, locally known as *hommel*. To celebrate that agrarian resurgence, the city of Poperinge hosts a triannual festival, complete with kids wearing hop-cone hats and the coronation of a hop queen. Created for the 1981 festival, the golden, honeyed Poperings Hommel is made with French malt, a yeast strain stretching back seven generations, and locally grown hops, including Hallertau, East Kent Goldings, and several undisclosed varieties. They lend a refined, flowery bouquet, a touch of citrus, and a spicy, herbal bitterness—terroir to a T.

FUN FACT: Van Eecke releases special editions of Poperings Hommel: one dry-hopped with local Saphir hops and another filled with fresh hops.

DERNIÈRE VOLONTÉ

DIEU DU CIEL! | ABV: 7%
MONTREAL, CANADA | AVAILABLE: YEAR-ROUND
DIEUDUCIEL.COM | GLASS: 🍷 | BITTERNESS: ★★☆☆

Founded in 1998, Dieu du Ciel! will have you crying "God in Heaven!" with their complex, stylistically goosed ales, which include the Rosée d'Hibiscus, a wheat beer tinted pink with hibiscus; Disco Soleil Kumquat IPA; and Route des Épices, a peppercorn-rocked rye beer. The hazy Dernière Volonté—French for "last will"—uses Belgian yeast for a fruity, zesty profile of peaches, apricots, and pepper that accords nicely with the floral hops and herbal bitterness.

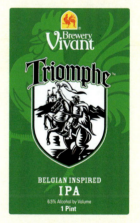

TRIOMPHE BELGIAN STYLE IPA

BREWERY VIVANT | ABV: 6.5%
GRAND RAPIDS, MICHIGAN | AVAILABLE: YEAR-ROUND
BREWERYVIVANT.COM | GLASS: 🍺🍷 | BITTERNESS: ★★☆☆

One of America's great beer cities, Grand Rapids is bubbling with grade-A bars, such as HopCat, and fantastic breweries, including Founders, Perrin, the Mitten, and Brewery Vivant. Located in a former funeral chapel, Vivant, the world's first LEED-certified brewery, takes inspiration from the time-tested farmhouse and monastic brewing traditions of France and Belgium, remixed for today's taste buds. Taste what I mean in the Big Red Coq, a crimson ale fermented with Belgian yeast and tropic-blasted with Citra and Saison. Tawny Triomphe, a terrific hybrid, stitches together classic Belgian aromatics (spice, cloves), subtle sweetness, an undercurrent of bitterness, and enough fruity, orangey goodness to raise the dead.

BREWERY SPOTLIGHT

BRUSSELS BEER PROJECT | BRUSSELS, BELGIUM ▮▮

Crowd-funded to life, this irreverently fresh brewery eschews dubbels, lambics, and tripels for en vogue ales such as the I Like It Bitter Double IPA made with varying hops; Babylone, partly brewed with stale supermarket bread and dry-hopped with Chinook; and Cheeky Kamille, a chamomile-infused pale ale. What did those investors get in exchange for their funding? Twelve bottles of beer a year for life.

DRINK: Delta, a tropical Belgian IPA and the brewery's first beer, as selected in a local competition.

When in Brussels, knock back sours and hop-focused brews at Moeder Lambic, a great bar with a location by the bronze *Manneken Pis* sculpture—which you might know better as the naked boy peeing into a fountain.

BROUWERIJ HOF TEN DORMAAL | TILDONK, BELGIUM ▮▮

On the family farm, former accountant André Janssens grows his own grains, hops, and fruit. He also sources his own yeast strains. The bona fide farmhouse brewery's agrarian-guided beers include Zure, a barrel-aged sour gone funky with native microflora, and White Gold, in which chicory root subs for hops. "In Belgium, it's tradition, tradition, tradition," Janssens says. "I don't believe in tradition. I believe in innovation."

DRINK: The Politician Farmhouse IPA, floral and bitter as an election.

BRETTANOMYCES IPAS

Yeast lurks everywhere we live. It hangs in the air we breathe, on the fruit we eat, and we stir it into our bread and brews. Not each strain makes great beer, though. Microbes are like people, wildly diverse with different skill sets. Sure, I can tell you what's worth tasting, but when it comes to writing computer code I might as well have been born fingerless. Some yeast strains throw off unwanted flavors or can't thrive in certain temperature ranges. To create consistent product, most breweries use commercially produced strains, mainly of the ale and lager variety. When those yeasts finish their sugary feast, they call it a job well done. *Brettanomyces*, however, is insatiable.

In science-speak (Greek), the word means "British fungus." Why? Danish scientist N. Hjelte Claussen identified it around 1903 from a soured English stock ale. It continually eats sugars, even tough-to-digest ones, to the bitter end, unlocking a secret cabinet of curious, unique flavors. Used for primary fermentation, Brett can throw off fruit-forward flavors veering toward tropical, perhaps mango or pineapple. Amplified by today's hops, these wild IPAs become fidgety, chameleonic creatures. The flavor profiles shift as hops fade and the yeast continues its work. When used alongside standard-issue *Saccharomyces* brewing yeast for secondary fermentation (bottle or barrel), Brett slowly dries a beer, imparting rustic flavors described as "funk," "barnyard," or the weirdly specific "horse blanket." Try a fresh wild IPA, and then compare it with one aged for six months. Only time can tell what the bottle will hold.

Drinker beware: Yeast harvested from Rogue brewmaster John Maier's facial follicles goes into the aptly named Beard Beer.

🌾 RED SWINGLINE IPA PRIMITIF

TRINITY BREWING COMPANY | ABV: 4.1%
COLORADO SPRINGS, COLORADO | AVAILABLE: ROTATING
TRINITYBREW.COM | GLASS: 🍷 | BITTERNESS: ★★★☆

Style classifications offer baseline expectations for what's bubbling beneath cap or cork, and Red Swingline makes for a categorization nightmare. First released in Trinity's *Office Space*–themed Case of the Mondays series, the session-strength "IPA primitif" uses coriander, tangerine, and a trio of fruity hops and ages in ex-Chardonnay French oak barrels spiked with souring *Lactobacillus* and *Brettanomyces*. Trinity also hits each barrel with dry hops. All of which makes this category-exploder as complex as they come: tart and lemony, evocative of pineapples and barnyard funk, and tannic for a wine-like finish. What to call Red Swingline? One word: sublime.

At the 2014 Festival of Barrel and Wood-Aged Beer in Chicago, Trinity secured silver in the wild/Brett category. Problem was, the beer contained no wild yeast. Founder Jason Yester graciously returned the medal . . . and then won silver for Red Swingline at the 2015 Great American Beer Festival.

🌾 HOP SAVANT

CROOKED STAVE ARTISAN BEER PROJECT | ABV: VARIES
DENVER, COLORADO | AVAILABLE: ROTATING
CROOKEDSTAVE.COM | GLASS: 🍷🍺 | BITTERNESS: ★★☆☆

No brewer has more drive to investigate the flavorful potential, and harness the untamed ferocity, of *Brettanomyces* than Chad Yakobson, who wrote his master's thesis on the subject. His scientific inquiries became Crooked Stave, where beers ferment with carefully collected and categorized strains before aging in oak. Every style goes wild—and often sour with added bacteria—from the seasonally shifting St. Bretta Witbier to Surette, a vinous, sustaining saison. Hop Savant encompasses an endless test specimen: brewed with Citra, Mosaic, and Simcoe hops; fermented with Brett cultures; dry-hopped with experimental varieties that make it tropical, funky, beguiling; and aged in oak foeders. The Hop Savant series also focuses on a single hop—Amarillo, say, or Galaxy—employed to glorious, aromatic excess.

FUN FACT: Every fall, Crooked Stave throws its wild What the Funk? festival in Denver.

🌾 EVOLVER IPA

WILD BEER CO. | ABV: 5.8%

SOMERSET, ENGLAND | AVAILABLE: ROTATING

WILDBEERCO.COM | GLASS: 🍺🍷 | BITTERNESS: ★★☆☆

To ensnare wild yeast, decamp to a bountiful locale, such as a fruit orchard, where unfermented wort, set out overnight, will attract the microscopic critters. Wild Beer, located close to Somerset's abundant apple orchards, produces the acidic, refreshing Somerset Wild and Champagne-like Ninkasi, which also courses with locally pressed apple juice. Brett goes into the Brits' bitter explorations, particularly the West Coast–inspired BrettBrett Double IPA and lower-potency Evolver, in which a hop sextet runs amok, including lemony Sorachi Ace and piney Chinook. Drink it young for a citric, tropical affair. Let it age for a drier, earthy funk.

FUN FACT: Founders Andrew Cooper and Brett Ellis decided to start Wild Beer after sampling Jolly Pumpkin's sour, barrel-aged La Roja at the Great British Beer Festival.

🌾 JUXTAPOSE BRETT IPA

FOUR WINDS BREWING | ABV: 6.5%

DELTA, CANADA | AVAILABLE: ROTATING

FOURWINDSBREWING.CA | GLASS: 🍷 | BITTERNESS: ★★☆☆

This brewery sits near the Fraser River, not far from the American border. That location becomes evident in the Zephyrus series, named for the Greek god of the western wind and focused on hop-centric beers so popular on the West Coast. Drink the Belgian-style Phaedra (Greek for "bright"), a beacon to wheat, rye, and Belma and Citra hops, and the tropical, hazy Apparition, fermented with witbier yeast. Juxtapose perches at the precipice of funk and fruit, evoking mangos and oranges served in a barnyard. No wonder the Canadian Brewing Awards named Four Winds its brewery of the year in 2015.

🌾 BRETT SESSION IPA

MICROBRASSERIE PIT CARIBOU | ABV: 4.5%

PERCÉ, QUÉBEC | AVAILABLE: ROTATING

PITCARIBOU.COM | GLASS: 🍺 | BITTERNESS: ★★☆☆

On the Gaspé Peninsula, where Québec meets the Gulf of St. Lawrence, you'll find Pit Caribou. Founded in 2007 and named for a rock formation, this Canadian brewery makes historically inspired Gaspesian beers, such as Blanche de Pratto, a witbier commemorating the 475th anniversary of explorer Jacques Cartier's arrival, and Gaspésienne No. 13, a robust porter. The cloudy Brett Session IPA tastes as piney and grapefruity as they come, fruitier and more tropical than you might expect, downplaying the funk in favor of bright, zesty refreshment.

FUN FACT: "Gaspé" comes from the Mi'kmaq word *gespe'g*, meaning "the end"—as in no more land.

BREWERY SPOTLIGHT

BRASSERIE DUNHAM | DUNHAM, QUÉBEC 🇨🇦

Located in wine and apple country, Brasserie Dunham has become one of Canada's creatively exhilarating breweries, doing right by wild ales and porters; rustic, raspberry, and hoppy saisons; and all manner of IPAs. Look for the Black IPA and its stronger version, plus Leo's Early Breakfast IPA, which contains Earl Grey tea and guava purée.

DRINK: Tropicale IPA, filled with wild yeast, summery mango and tangerine, and Mandarina Bavaria hops.

⬛ FLAVORED ⬛

The clamor around IPAs can prove deafening, everyone shouting at the same IBU pitch. To sing a different tune, brewers are adulterating IPAs with vegetables and fruit in perfect harmony with citrusy hops. A sprinkle of pepper, a good tea steep, or a coffee bean rendezvous gives these brews a unique timbre and will resonate with drinkers seeking something new, yet familiar. Post-production tweaks are becoming popular as well. For example: aging in ex-bourbon or ex-Chardonnay barrels provides unexpected and appealing flavor notes. Palm your pint glass, and prepare your palate for a flavorful new experience.

WOOD-AGED IPAS

Before technology made life modern, all beer aged in wood. Casks, tanks, and barrels seasoned lagers, stouts, and IPAs alike, mellowing them and contributing tannic complexity. The mass production of the twentieth century largely did away with that practice, but what's old is once again new. Brewers are using wooden vessels for stouts, which find affinity in barrels that once held bourbon, as well as sours that waltz with transformative microbes in wooden chambers.

Today's IPAs rarely interact with wood. Brewers construct them for swift consumption not for months-long lounging and losing their oomph, right? Mostly, yes. Some stronger IPAs can withstand, and even find improvement in, a wood nap or infusion with timber, such as poplar or cedar. Gigantic and Saint Arnold both age IPAs in gin barrels, while Breakside opted for aquavit. In 2015, Sierra Nevada collaborated with Stone to create NxS IPA, a blend of beers aged in ex-rye barrels, ex-bourbon barrels infused with gin, and fresh barrels. That seriously dry-hopped IPA has taste layers like tiramisu, so let's get splintered.

HITACHINO NEST JAPANESE CLASSIC ALE

KIUCHI BREWERY | ABV: 7%
NAKA, JAPAN | AVAILABLE: YEAR-ROUND
KODAWARI.CC | GLASS: 🍺 | BITTERNESS: ★★☆☆

In 1823, village honcho Kiuchi Gihei founded a brewery to produce sake and distill shochu. The Kiuchi company started brewing beer in 1996, two years after Japan's government altered the laws that prevented small breweries from operating. Their Hitachino Nest beers marry peerless craftsmanship to native ingredients. Standouts include the pink-hued Red Rice Ale; Dai Dai IPA, flavored with wild Fukure Mikan mandarins; and the Saison du Japon, which contains koji, or malted rice, used for making sake. The Classic Ale re-creates a nineteenth-century style aged specifically in cedar. It has a semi-sweet stew of spice and wood, caramelized apples, and mild, yet insistent bitterness.

Following the catastrophic Tōhoku earthquake and tsunami in 2011, Kiuchi lost power for three days, allowing a witbier mash to start fermenting. They named the result 3 Days and released 8,000 bottles the following year.

🌾 HOPANOMALY

NEBRASKA BREWING COMPANY | ABV: 10.6%

PAPILLION, NEBRASKA | AVAILABLE: ROTATING

NEBRASKABREWINGCO.COM | GLASS: 🍷 | BITTERNESS: ★★★☆

Founding NBC in this pint-size city in 2007, husband and wife Paul and Kim Kavulak have redefined beer in both the Cornhusker State and America. You'll love the Cardinal Pale Ale, copiously dry-hopped with Cascade, and the West Coast–style IPA awash with aromas of citrus and pine trees. It's their aptitude with barrel-aging, however, that put them on the map. The Reserve Series includes Mélange à Trois, a strong Belgian-style blonde aged in ex-Chardonnay barrels, and Apricot au Poivre, a saison seasoned with black pepper and apricot purée and aged in ex-wine barrels. HopAnomaly starts as a spicy, tropical, citrusy Belgian-style IPA, then spends six months sleeping in ex-Chardonnay barrels, which add lush and lovely notes of vanilla and tannic oak.

FUN FACT: Known originally as Hop God, HopAnomaly's base version is often available on draft.

ᛘ HOPLAR

HARDYWOOD PARK CRAFT BREWERY | ABV: 8.5%

RICHMOND, VIRGINIA | AVAILABLE: EARLY SPRING

HARDYWOOD.COM | GLASS: 🍷 | BITTERNESS: ★★★☆

From the strange sours of Strangeways to Stone's first East Coast outpost, the erstwhile capital of the Confederacy has become a brewing powerhouse. One of its stars, Hardywood makes especially good IPAs, including the resin-charged, grapefruity Great Return and imperial-strength Hoplar. To make this mahogany beer, they toast Virginia poplar, which seasons a solidly bitter IPA powered by Columbus, Summit, and Cascade. You'll taste caramel, resinous pine, and a sprinkling of earth needled with tannins, and it's gangbusters with grilled meat.

FUN FACT: In 2011, Hardywood debuted the annual wet-hopped RVA IPA, using hops grown by local residents. It's like drinking Richmond by the pint.

🌾 KENTUCKY RYE BARREL IPA

ALLTECH LEXINGTON BREWING AND DISTILLING CO. | ABV: 10%
LEXINGTON, KENTUCKY | AVAILABLE: SPRING
KENTUCKYALE.COM | GLASS: 🍷🍷 | BITTERNESS: ★★☆☆

This global biotech firm focuses on animal feed, crop health, and, starting in 1999, brewing and distilling. That might seem like a strange leap, but Irish-born founder Pearse Lyons earned his doctorate in brewing and distilling and previously worked for Harp Lager and Irish Distillers, who make Jameson Irish whiskey. Yeast forms the beating heart of Alltech's business, deployed in the Town Branch line of rye and bourbon and its collection of bourbon-barreled brews, encompassing stouts, pumpkin ales, and IPAs. Aged in freshly emptied Town Branch rye and Kentucky bourbon barrels, this imperial IPA drinks more vibrant and citrus-charged than you'd expect, spooned with classic spice and vanilla crème brûlée.

When in Lexington, visit the Bread Box, a former Rainbo Bread factory retrofitted to include a hydroponic plant and fish farm (supplying the on-site Smithtown Seafood restaurant), Bluegrass Distillers, and West Sixth Brewing, which makes a piney, peachy IPA and a lemongrass-spiced wheat ale.

BREWERY SPOTLIGHT

FERAL BREWING CO. | BASKERVILLE, AUSTRALIA 🇦🇺

Since 2002, this brewery has made beers both tame (Belgian-style White, Sly Fox Summer Ale) and wildly flavorful, such as the sour Watermelon Warhead Berliner Weisse, aged in ex-Chardonnay barrels. The immensely popular Hop Hog squeals with citrus. Also try the dark and rich Karma Citra and the annual Tusk Imperial IPA.

DRINK: Barrel Fermented Hog, their best-selling IPA, fermented in fresh French oak barriques.

CITRUS, VEGETABLE & SPICED IPAS

Nature's seemingly limitless bounty of fruit, vegetables, and seasonings increasingly is finding its way into IPAs, creating beers that scramble shelving rules at grocery stores. Stone made the collaborative Japanese Green Tea IPA; Smog City blends the evolving Grape Ape IPA with different varieties of fruit; and hibiscus flowers turn Night Shift Brewing's JoJo IPA pink.

To embellish an IPA's inherent hop flavors of citrus, brewers are adding juicy rushes, including peel or zest, of grove-fresh lemons and limes, oranges and grapefruit. Refreshers such as Burnt Hickory's Didjits Blood Orange IPA, Abita's Grapefruit Harvest IPA, and Funky Buddha's Funky Buddha More Moro Blood Orange IPA contain rays of sunshine in their bottles, brightening moods all year round. Here are six great flavored IPAs from brewers who know how to use an infusion.

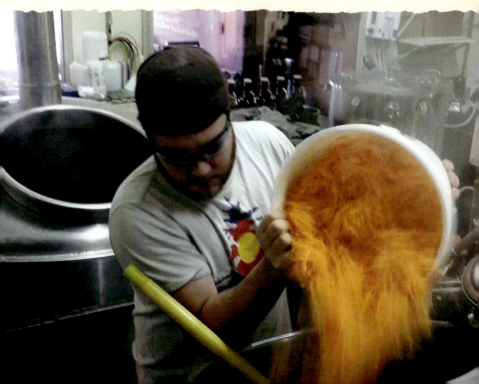

ROOTS REVIVAL CARROT IPA

TWISTED PINE BREWING CO. | ABV: 7.2%
BOULDER, COLORADO | AVAILABLE: ROTATING
TWISTEDPINEBREWING.COM | GLASS: 🍺 | BITTERNESS: ★★☆☆

Whether it's the agave nectar that gives their Agaveras IPA incredibly light body or the incendiary ghost chile peppers that turn Ghost Face Killah into a carbonated flamethrower, Twisted Pine knows from esoteric, unlikely ingredients. Their Farm to Foam series celebrates Colorado's agricultural bounty in liquid form. Releases include: Bramble On, a boysenberry-filled Belgian-style blonde ale; briskly refreshing Cucumber Cream Ale; and the Roots Revival Carrot IPA, which features locally sown wheat and barley, Colorado-grown Cascade and Crystal hops, and 300 pounds of fresh carrots. The veggies supply a touch of earth on the nose and light sweetness, working in concert with the citrus and mild bitterness.

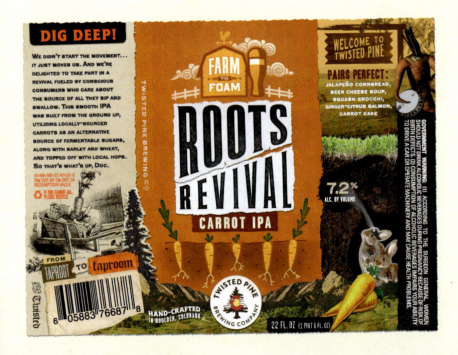

🌾 SLICED NECTARINE IPA

MOODY TONGUE | ABV: 5.9%

CHICAGO, ILLINOIS | AVAILABLE: YEAR-ROUND

MOODYTONGUE.COM | GLASS: 🍺 | BITTERNESS: ★★☆☆

"We're pushing down the walls of culinary arts and brewing," says founder Jared Rouben, and he means it. At Moody Tongue, the Culinary Institute of America grad and Goose Island veteran builds layers of flavor by sourcing farmers' market–fresh ingredients, determining how best to highlight their tastes and aromatics, then incorporating them during brewing. That means brandying purple raspberries for his Belgian dubbel, using Oaxacan cacao in the Caramelized Chocolate Churro Baltic Porter, and sourcing rare Australian truffles for the clean-drinking, beguilingly complex Shaved Black Truffle Pilsner. The Sliced Nectarine IPA doesn't launch a full-bore fruit assault but rather offers a layered expression of stonefruit and understated caramel, citrusy aromatics, and a moderately bitter finish.

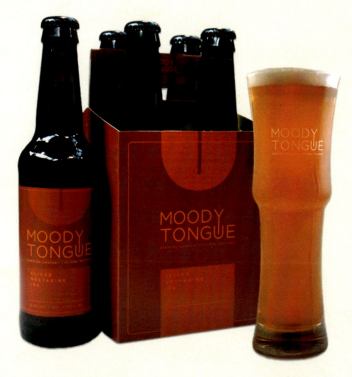

🌾 JUICY TREE

SHORT'S BREWING COMPANY | ABV: 7.5%

BELLAIRE, MICHIGAN | AVAILABLE: NOVEMBER

SHORTSBREWING.COM | GLASS: 🍺 | BITTERNESS: ★★☆☆

If you like boozy desserts, you're going to love Short's brews. Their culinary-inspired beers include Key Lime Pie, Strawberry Short's Cake, and both S'more and PB&J stouts. They also shine with the Belgian-style Pan Galactic Gargle Blaster Double IPA (tip of the hat to Douglas Adams) and the Huma Lupa Licious IPA, "a complex hop and malt theme park in your mouth." Think of Juicy Tree as a Christmas IPA made by a gin-loving arborist. Hops, blue spruce tips, juniper berries, and cranberries mob the beer, blending the tartness and fruit sweetness with evergreen bitterness.

FUN FACT: In 2016, Short's expanded their distribution from just Michigan to include Indiana, Illinois, and Ohio.

🌾 AVATAR JASMINE IPA

ELYSIAN BREWING COMPANY | ABV: 6.3%

SEATTLE, WASHINGTON | AVAILABLE: YEAR-ROUND

ELYSIANBREWING.COM | GLASS: 🍺 | BITTERNESS: ★★☆☆

Elysian's IPA collection includes modern constructs, such as Dayglow, agog with wheat, Mosaic, and El Dorado, and the Space Dust Double IPA, hit with Citra and Amarillo. Jasmine flowers give the orange-gold Avatar—the Hindu term for an earthly incarnation of a god—its intense perfume-worthy aromatics. Don't think potpourri, though. Toasty, bready sweetness mingles with the floral, citrusy flavors among moderate bitterness. It's East meets best.

🌾 PINK IPA

BIRRIFICIO ALMOND '22 | ABV: 6.2%

PESCARA, ITALY | AVAILABLE: YEAR-ROUND

BIRRAALMOND.COM | GLASS: 🍺 | BITTERNESS: ★★☆☆

In the hills along the Adriatic Coast directly across from Rome, you'll find a factory where women create sugared almonds. Almond '22 continues this culinary focus with unpasteurized, unfiltered, delicately bottle-conditioned beers that pull liberally from the kitchen cabinet. Chestnut honey and orange zest flavor the smoky Torbata, inspired by single-malt Scotch, and Farrotta stars spelt and honey from local beekeepers. This cloudy golden "Italian pale ale" contains Brazilian pink pepper for a pleasantly spicy finish. Nelson Sauvin hops supply a tropical, fruity bouquet complemented by grapefruit zest, while German hops impart a grassy bitterness. One taste and you'll be tickled, yes, pink.

🌾 ART LA INDIANA

ART CERVESERS | ABV: 6.2%

CANOVELLES, SPAIN | AVAILABLE: YEAR-ROUND

ARTCERVESERS.COM | GLASS: 🍺 | BITTERNESS: ★★☆☆

Located near Barcelona, Art Cervesers ("Brewers Art") aims to revive traditional brewing techniques, creating thoroughly Spanish beers that celebrate indigenous culture and ingredients. The Coure Winter Ale contains nutmeg and Myrica gale, and they brew a banana-scented hefeweizen with local spelt. Categorized as a "Catalan IPA," Art La Indiana resulted from a year of recipe refinement. Carob powder, a traditional cocoa substitute, gives the creamy brew a garnet hue and a chocolaty taste that complements the citrusy, fruity flavor and fragrance. It's unusually delicious.

BREWERY SPOTLIGHT

BAIRD BREWING | IZU (AND ELSEWHERE), JAPAN 🔴

"Balance + complexity = character" expresses the winning formula for Baird Beer, founded in 2000 by husband and wife Bryan and Sayuri Baird. They make impeccably calibrated pale ales; IPAs, such as the Rising Sun Pale Ale and Suruga Bay Imperial IPA; beers incorporating native fruit (Temple Garden Yuzu Ale, Carpenter's Mikan Ale); and spot-on classics, including the Shuzenji Heritage Helles.

DRINK: the Fruitful Life Citrus IPA, flavored with daidai, an Asian bitter orange

BREWSKI | HELSINGBORG, SWEDEN 🇸🇪

Marcus Hjalmarsson ditched his window-cleaning company to start this brewery, which focuses on outré formulations that rely heavily on fruit, including pineapple pale ales and mango-packed IPAs, plus Passionate Beating, a Berliner weisse flavored with passion fruit and beets.

DRINK: Mangofebeer, a fruity double IPA lavishly dosed with mango.

CERVEJARIA BODEBROWN | CURITIBA, BRAZIL 🇧🇷

A six hour drive southeast of São Paulo, Bodebrown doubles as a beer school (tasting, pairing, brewing classes) and a brewery fusing tradition to innovation. They do Scotch ales classically and stuffed with cacao, IPAs imperial and darkly rye-driven, tripels agog with grains of paradise, and hefeweizens dry-hopped with Amarillo.

DRINK: Cacau IPA, a collaboration with Stone that twins citrusy hops to cocoa nibs.

COFFEE IPAS

Adding coffee to an IPA might seem like a major-league mistake. After all, coffee beans frequently shack up with stouts and porters. Like meets like. As with malt, however, not every coffee bean need taste like a four-alarm fire. With climate consideration and different processing techniques, growers worldwide are creating beans with vast biodiversity, and roasters can control intensity. All of which creates unexpected flavors.

As my coffee expert pal Erin Meister writes, drying the cascara, or outer cherry, before removing it creates fruity, berry-like flavors, but undress the coffee bean right away and you'll create floral notes, perhaps evoking lemongrass. (Denver Beer Co. and Kent Falls have created cascara IPAs.) Don't believe it? Check out the tasting notes at your local gourmet coffee shop, or hit Chicago's annual Uppers & Downers, a celebration of coffee and beer thrown by Good Beer Hunting and Intelligentsia Coffee.

Fruity and floral . . . sound familiar? By using low-acidity cold brew or steeping beans like tea, brewers are creating coffee IPAs high in hop-matching flavor and aroma but low in astringency, as in FATE Brewing's Moirai Coffee IPA, Captain Lawrence's Stumptown cold brew–infused Hopsomaniac IPA, and Mikkeller's ingredient-rotating Koppi Coffee IPAs. Other breweries take coffee IPAs to the dark side, as with Brodies Chinook Black Coffee Black IPA. The caffeine won't jolt you like an espresso, but these coffee IPAs are definitely buzz-worthy.

🌾 COFFEE IPA

BEANERY BREWING | ABV: 6%
WOODSTOCK, VERMONT | AVAILABLE: ROTATING
FACEBOOK.COM/BEANERYBREWING | GLASS: 🥃 | BITTERNESS: ★★☆☆

"We want to expand the flavor palette of beer," Dave Brodrick says in Blind Tiger Ale House, his agenda-setting New York City beer bar. At Beanery, Brodrick and Dave Yarrington, Smuttynose's former brewmaster, team up with CQ Coffee Roasters' Claudia Barrett to create beers that roastily flout expectations. The Latte Stout stars sun-dried, briefly fermented Indonesian beans redolent of strawberries and bourbon, and the Coffee IPA has a dark-gold tint with a bouquet of citrus and pine. Complementing both are Costa Rican beans that magically create flavors of lemons and brown sugar—coffee like you least expect it.

FUN FACT: Brodrick also co-owns Vermont's Worthy Burger.

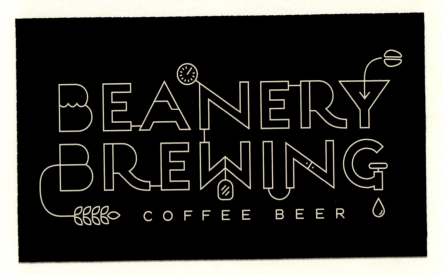

BLACK MALTS & BODY SALTS BLACK COFFEE IIPA

TO ØL | ABV: 9.9%

COPENHAGEN, DENMARK | AVAILABLE: YEAR-ROUND

TO-OL.DK | GLASS: 🍷🍷 | BITTERNESS: ★★★☆

A gypsy outfit run by maverick buddies Tobias Emil Jensen and Tore Gynther, To Øl ("two beers" in Danish) focuses on flavorful provocations, such as the funky, farmhouse-style Fuck Art This Is Architecture and Mine Is Bigger Than Yours barley wine. Their coal-black, lightly oily, multifaceted, imperial-strength IPA, teeming with French press coffee and mountains of hops, conjures espresso and smoke, lemon zest and pine trees, along with flavors of berries and dark chocolate. Body salts—because obviously you're wondering—are drops of brewer's sweat that accidentally fall into a brew kettle.

FUN FACT: Alcohol is antiseptic.

🌾 JAVA THE HOP

FORT GEORGE BREWERY | ABV: 6.5%

ASTORIA, OREGON | AVAILABLE: WINTER

FORTGEORGEBREWERY.COM | GLASS: 🍺 | BITTERNESS: ★★☆☆

For most IPA-centric breweries, single-hop beers set the standard, but an IPA featuring one hop *and* coffee bean? Yes, please! Java the Hop—which deserves an award for best *Star Wars* pun—unites woodsy Simcoe with Coava Coffee Roaster's Gichuna, a Kenyan bean with notes of caramel, molasses, hibiscus, and rhubarb. Overall, the vibrant orange mash-up tastes harmoniously of pine trees topped with caramelized vanilla and citrus, with bitterness supplied by both costars. Also try Fort George's other IPAs, including the floral, piney Vortex and the Fresh IPA, made with just-harvested Mosaic hops.

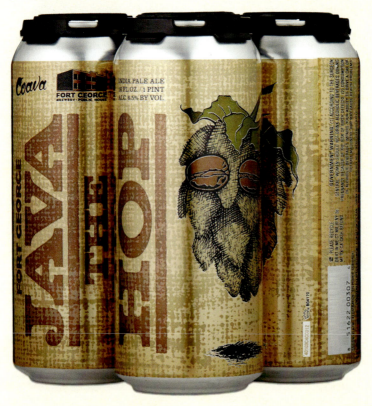

BREWERY SPOTLIGHT

WEIRD BEARD BEER CO. | LONDON, ENGLAND 🇬🇧

Uncompromising, nonconformist, genre-exploding friends Bryan Spooner and Gregg Irwin—prodigiously hirsute and talented homebrewers gone pro—pour out their Faithless Spreadsheet Ninja Black Pilsner, tart You Taste Better When You Are Scared grapefruit IPA, and Little Things That Kill, a session pale ale smoothed with oats and lactose. Expect the unexpected.

DRINK: Out of Office, brewed with Ethiopian coffee beans that impart a blueberry flavor.

⇥ SOUR & UNUSUAL ⇤

Until recently, if an IPA tasted tongue-curlingly sour or funkier than French cheese, someone seriously screwed up. Now some brewers are aiming for that taste. They're dry-hopping tart, sour beers like the dickens, creating aromatic quenchers that rival lemonade for refreshment. That might seem strange, but wait . . . there's more! Other adventurous IPA makers are gassing their brews with nitrogen—a move often reserved to Guinness and other stouts—as well as spiking them with fiery peppers or hemp extract. Go on, give these oddballs a sip.

DRY-HOPPED SOURS

Like IPAs, sours are on the rise, so it was only a matter of time before the two styles crossed wires to create a crushable mash-up: the dry-hopped sour. Tart and refreshing, lip-tingling and intensely aromatic, the hybrid works so well because of science. Typically, hop aroma fades quickly, but an acidic environment helps preserve the bouquet, creating a liquid time capsule. (The acids also can alter hop flavor—for better or worse.) New Belgium trailblazed the technique with their Le Terroir Dry-Hopped Sour Ale, but the fusion is growing worldwide. Oregon's Breakside makes the tropically hopped La Tormenta, and Denver's Baere Brewing cooks up a range of dry-hopped table sours. Chorlton Brewing in England does multiple dry-hopped sour pales, as does Danish gypsy brewer To Øl alongside dry-hopped sour IPAs in its Sur line. Buckle up for an acid trip.

🌾 LE TERROIR

NEW BELGIUM BREWING COMPANY | ABV: 7.5%
FORT COLLINS, COLORADO | AVAILABLE: FALL
NEWBELGIUM.COM | GLASS: 🍷 | BITTERNESS: ★☆☆☆

In 2003, Lauren Salazar couldn't figure out what to do with Felix, a wood-aged sour beer. The solution lay in Amarillo—which Darren Gamache had discovered growing wild on his family's Washington farm in 1997—and its novel floral, citrusy profile that hinted at mangos and peaches, the same flavors as Felix. "I love hop selection, I love the aroma of hops, I love everything about hops except for bitterness," says Salazar, now New Belgium's specialty brand manager. "I thought, *Why do hops have to be bitter?* They don't." She dry-hopped Felix with Amarillo, which led to Le Terroir, a reference to the beer's foudres, or wooden aging tanks. Now matched with a different hop each year, Le Terroir lays out tropical fruit, peaches, melons mixed with citrus, and a terrific counterbalancing tartness. "Just like an IPA, you can't stop smelling it," says Salazar. "You have to tell yourself to stop smelling it and take a drink."

FUN FACT: New Belgium's draft-only Hop Kitchen series features experimental beers such as the hazy Juicy Mandarina IPA, herbaceous Botanical Imperial IPA, and tropical-sour Hop Tart.

🌾 SUPER GOING

GRIMM ARTISANAL ALES | ABV: 4.8%

BROOKLYN, NEW YORK | AVAILABLE: SUMMER

GRIMMALES.COM | GLASS: 🍷 | BITTERNESS: ★☆☆☆

Spouses Joe (musician) and Lauren (artist) turned their ardor for home-brewing into a thrillingly adventurous, nomadic brewing company that has embraced the smooth, plush grandeur of new-breed Northeast double IPAs; imperial stouts, including the Double Negative, which won GABF gold; and lavishly dry-hopped sours. Try the wild, mind-bending Psychokinesis, which will move your soul (and taste buds) with Mosaic and El Dorado. Their two tart, dry-hopped, oak-conditioned goses are perfect for summer sipping. Hit with lemon zest, Super Symmetry gets its tropical pluck from American hops, while its twin, Super Going, goes for orange zest and Mandarina Bavaria and Hull Melon hops from Germany.

ETERNAL SUNSHINE

PIZZA BOY BREWING | ABV: 5.2%
ENOLA, PENNSYLVANIA | AVAILABLE: YEAR-ROUND
PIZZABOYBREWING.COM | GLASS: 🍷 | BITTERNESS: ★☆☆☆

Across the Susquehanna from Harrisburg, you'll find Al's of Hampden, a pizzeria with its own brewery, Pizza Boy, the latest brewground for sour savant Terry Hawbaker. In the mid-Aughts, he head-brewed at central Pennsylvania's Bullfrog, building a national rep for his saisons, sours, and wild ales, including the barrel-seasoned, honey-hit Beekeeper, which won gold at the GABF. At Pizza Boy, he hammers out great IPAs, such as the dry, well-hopped West Shore and spicy Simcoe SamuRYE. Wilds and sours have pride of place, too, especially the dry-hopped Eternal Sunshine,

bright gold, citrusy, tropical, and invigoratingly tart but not mouth-twisting. Also worth your while: Hawbaker's solo Intangible Ales line of wild yeast wonders.

FUN FACT: Intangible collaborated with Evil Twin to create Sour Bikini, a scantily boozy, dry-hopped sour session ale.

BREWERY SPOTLIGHT

CHORLTON BREWING CO. | MANCHESTER, ENGLAND 🇬🇧

German brewing traditions, interpreted for modern times, guide Chorlton, which lies beneath a Manchester railway arch. Their unfiltered, unpasteurized beers include the Citra Brett Pale, fermented with yeast harvested from old German beer bottles, such as a Berliner weisse from 1977, and sours dry-hopped with contemporary hops, including Waimea, Citra, and Ahtanum.

DRINK: Amarillo Sour, fermented with *Lactobacillus* and British yeast, jacked with juicy Vic Secret and Amarillo hops, and canned.

NEW FRONTIERS

Each week brings news of a new IPA crossing further boundaries of experimentation. Some are daring, as with Ballast Point Sculpin IPA, which uses habaneros to create a tropical heat-seeker. Others simply *dare* you to drink them. 3 Sheeps Brewing's experimental IPA gets its inky tint from, yeah, squid ink; Dad & Dudes, which operates in 420-friendly Colorado, infuses one of their IPAs with cannabidiol; and Figueroa Mountain packs its Hoppy Poppy IPA with poppy seeds, the plant source for heroin and other opiates. As long as IPAs continue their rocket-ship ascent, brewers will keep monkeying with the template, seeking out the next great ingredient or technique—or just the one that lands them the most press. Either way, meet the new generation of offbeat IPAs.

NITRO IPA

GUINNESS | ABV: 5.8%

DUBLIN, IRELAND | AVAILABLE: YEAR-ROUND

GUINNESS.COM | GLASS: 🍺 | BITTERNESS: ★☆☆☆

The nitrogen that gives Guinness stout its creamy, milkshake qualities also flattens aroma, bitterness, and carbonation—three essential hallmarks of the modern IPA—so at first blush this Irish IPA seemed like a trend-chasing gimmick. The bubbles that cascaded into a creamy chef's cap pleasantly proved me wrong, however. Nitro IPAs probably aren't the future

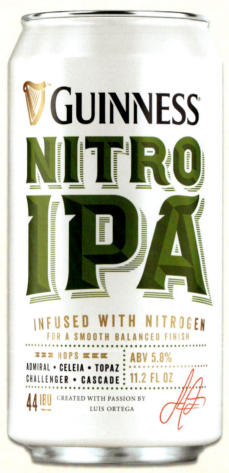

of the category—even though Sam Adams and Breckenridge now offer a tasty nitro line that includes an IPA—but truth be told: They're pretty tasty. If you favor liquid aggression, though, you'll sip disappointment. The gassed-up Guinness IPA makes for an appealing understatement in which muted citrus and pine needles flutter across the tongue.

FUN FACT: Guinness also operates Open Gate, an experimental small-batch brewery worth visiting.

WELCOME TO SCOVILLE

JAILBREAK BREWING COMPANY | ABV: 6.9%
LAUREL, MARYLAND | AVAILABLE: YEAR-ROUND
JAILBREAKBREWING.COM | GLASS: 🍺 | BITTERNESS: ★★☆☆

In a hot mango salsa, the tropical sweetness of the fruit blends with the intense scorch of peppers. Now translate that formula to beer. There's something to be said for the masochistic delights of a spicy IPA. In Welcome to Scoville, named for the scale that measures spicy heat, Jailbreak combines jalapeños and cilantro in a crash-up that tastes more vegetal than incendiary. It burns low but never overwhelms. (For an even more fiery IPA, try Ballast Point's lip-singeing Habanero Sculpin.)

If Scoville tastes like dullsville and you can gulp the Habanero Sculpin with ease, go for Twisted Pine's Ghost Face Killah, made with the ghost pepper, one of the world's hottest, which registers at more than 1 million Scoville units!

🌾 SATIVA IPA

DAD & DUDES BREWERIA | ABV: 6.5%
AURORA, COLORADO | AVAILABLE: ROTATING
BREWERIA.COM | GLASS: 🍺 | BITTERNESS: ★★☆☆

Founded in 2010, Dad & Dudes made a splash with their Dank IPA, Sativa IPA, and Indica Double IPA. To remain legal, the father-son brewery's Canna-Beer series doesn't contain any THC. The beers feature cannabidiol, a non-psychoactive hemp extract. Sativa sips at a relatively modest session strength, while the Indica Double tastes like a college dorm room in liquid form.

BREWERY SPOTLIGHT

GARAGE PROJECT | WELLINGTON, NEW ZEALAND

Friends Jos Ruffell and Ian Gillespie, with Ian's brother, Pete, as head brewer, started 50 flavorful liters at a time: Pernicious Weed, an imperial redolent of white wine and grapefruit; Amarillo-packed Angry Peaches IPA; and food-inspired brews, such as Cookies & Cream and Cereal Milk Stout. They rarely repeat beers, so drink 'em while you can.

DRINK: Death from Above, made with mango, hot peppers, and Vietnamese mint.

Added to beer, lactose supplies sweetness, body, and more sugars for fermentation. Usually associated with milk stouts, lactose contributes creamy textural complexity to beers such as 3 Floyds' Apocalypse Cow Double IPA, Tired Hands' fruited Milkshake IPAs, and Against the Grain's Booby Trap.

ACKNOWLEDGMENTS

Life tests limits. How far can you stretch your rubber band of sanity before it snaps, whacking you in the kisser? Answer: Write a book in fewer than four months as your daughter enters her terrible twos, your dog develops abandonment issues, your wife returns to work full-time, and your landlord sells your home of thirteen years out from under you, forcing you to find a new apartment and move on December 30. Ladies and gentlemen, my rubber band nearly broke, but scads of IPAs—in bottles, cans, growlers—helped me keep it together. Definitely not doctor-recommended, but it worked, as did the support from Team Sterling, in particular my editor, James Jayo, and photo editor, Stacey Stambaugh, for her image-hunting prowess and tenacity. Kudos also go to Gavin Motnyk for the interior design and Elizabeth Lindy, who crushed the cover.

My fellow beer writers Justin Kennedy, Joe Wiebe, Crystal Luxmore, Reid Ramsay, Ken Weaver, and Matt Curtis deserve many IPAs for helping me hone the list of those that appear in this book. Beer-pairing maestro Adam Dulye deserves a week of dinners for ensuring that my couplings didn't taste like car crashes. I'll also lay down a credit card for rounds with all the brewers who took the time to talk, impart advice, and let me tell their stories. The IPA revolution stands on the shoulders of your hop-filled wort and hard work.

Huge hugs and kisses to my daughter, Violet, for dragging me happily into a toddler's world of curiosity and giggling joy. That goes double for my wife, Jenene, who helped me not go cuckoo when, sleep-deprived and googly-eyed, I sought yet more synonyms for citrus and pine.

TOP FIVE IPAS (BY VOLUME)
CONSUMED WHILE WRITING *COMPLETE IPA*

1. Sierra Nevada Celebration Ale
2. Founders All Day IPA
3. Bell's Two Hearted Ale
4. Ballast Point Sculpin IPA
5. Evil Twin Intangible Ales Sour Bikini

IMAGE CREDITS

THE AUTHOR AND PUBLISHER THANK ALL OF THE BREWERIES AND INDIVIDUALS WHO PROVIDED IMAGES FOR USE IN THIS BOOK.

All images copyright of the corresponding breweries with the following additions: II-III: © Grit City Photography/Bale Breaker Brewing Company; IX: Tod Seelie; X: © Brouwerij Van Eecke; 2: © Alastair Philip Wiper/The Kernel Brewery; 7: © Alltech Lexington Brewing and Distilling; 9: © Bree Tait/Epic Brewing Company; 10, 15: © Grit City Photography/Bale Breaker Brewing Company; 11: Courtesy Wikimedia Foundation; 18: © *Brew By Numbers*; 22: © Isaac Newman/Beavertown Brewery; 27: © Mikkel Borg Bjergsø/Mikkeller; 28: © Brew Dog; 30, 42: © Sam Needham/Magic Rock Brewing; 34 top, 35: © Alastair Philip Wiper/The Kernel Brewery; 34 bottom: © Michael Kelly/The Kernel Brewery; 43: © Jon Page; 46, 49: © Peter Jensen Bissell/Bissell Brothers; 50, 68, 92, 110, 130: © Map Resources; 52: © Fair Folk/Trillium Brewing Company; 53: © Bob M. Montgomery Images 2016/Hill Farmstead Brewery; 55: © Tyler Finck/Ithaca Beer Co.; 56, 57: © Samantha Fisch/Stoneface Brewing Company; 59: © SweetWater Brewing Company; 61: © Russell Breslow/Cigar City Brewing; 62: © Jake Wagner/Port City Brewing; 66: © Mike Carroll/NoDa Brewing Company; 67: © Ray Goodrich/Foothills Brewing; 70: © Studio Schulz/Terrapin Beer Company; 72: © Rich Tarbell/Champion Brewing; 73, 76: © Jonathan Reynolds/Rhinegeist; 85: © Great Divide Brewery; 91: © Scott Wood/Snake River Brewery; 96 bottom: © John Holzer; 97, 99: © Michela Ricci/Arizona Wilderness Brewing Co.; 101: © Reid Ramsay/Beer Street Journal; 107: © *Coronado Brewing* Company; 91: © Brian Doll/AleSmith Brewing; 102, 103: © Patrick Darby Photography/SanTan Brewing Company; 104 top: © Annie Ray/Alpine Beer Company; 113: © Mike V. Sardina/Societe Brewing Company; 114 right: © Beachwood BBQ; 116: © Suni Sidhu/@instapint/Cellarmaker Brewing Company; 117: © John Storey; 121, 126, 127: © Baker County Tourism/Barley Brown's Beer; 123: © Blind Tiger Design/Bale Breaker Brewing Company; 124: © Matt Mioduszewski/Hopworks; 129 right: © Tim LaBarge/Gigantic Brewing Company; 132 right: © Daria Stein/Ecliptic Brewing; 134: © Greg Von Doersten/Melvin Brewing; 136, 155: © The Boston Beer Company; 143: © Gustav Karlsson Frost/Omnipollo; 145: © Studio Schulz/Port Brewing Company; 146, 147: © Greg Von Doersten/Melvin Brewing; 148: © Nicole Irwin & Jeff Giampaolo/Fiddlehead Brewing; 150: © Eric Heinig/BrewCT.com; 158 right: © Carmen Vicente/Bellwoods Brewery; 162: © *Dogfish Head* Craft Brewery; 168, 169: © Matt Coats/Other Half Brewing Company; 172: © Digiman Studio (photo), Butler Creative (label)/Knee Deep Brewing Company; 176: © Justin Schau, Brewer/Southern Tier Brewing Co.; 181: © Brian Casse; 182: © Brian Stechschulte/Speakeasy; 188: © Matthew Curtis; 191 top: © Zach Thoren, Associate Brand Manager/Southern Tier Brewing Co.; 194: © Jennifer Balcombe/Camden Town Brewery; 196: © Samantha Fisch/Stoneface Brewing Company; 204: © Courtland Wells/Southern Prohibition Brewing; 208 top: © Sasquatch Agency/Widmer Brothers Brewing 246: © Michael Dieterle/CraftBeerMonger.com/*Trinity Brewing* Company; 249: © Alison Page/Four Winds Brewing Company; 257: © Twisted Pine Brewing Company; 258: © Anthem Branding/Twisted Pine Brewing Company; 273: © Jailbreak Brewing Company; 276: © Aaron Bitters ABI LLC/Dads & Dudes Breweria

IPA FESTIVALS

These days, you only have to drive to your local supermarket, beer shop, or brewery to find a first-rate IPA, but if you want to sip dozens of them, each as fresh as the day they left the fermenter, earmark a couple of days for a beer festival. Festivals once assembled dozens of disparate styles, a smorgasbord of cream ale and kölsch, saison and stout. Now they're focusing on single concepts, such as sours, barrel-aged beers, and, yes, IPAs. Mark your calendar, pack your bags, and head to these hopped-up celebrations across America and around the globe.

Dates and participating breweries may change for each festival.
Consult the websites for up-to-date information.

AMERICA

CALIFORNIA

The Bistro Double IPA Festival, Hayward, February | the-bistro.com
Founded in 2000 and held in conjunction with San Francisco Beer Week, this festival features nearly 100 of the best double and triple IPAs that the West Coast can offer.

Festival of Dankness, San Diego, August | moderntimesbeer.com
Primo IPA purveyors Modern Times organize this head-blowing collection of the globe's most covetable IPA breweries. Past participants include Knee Deep, Half Acre, and New Zealand's Garage Project.

Single, Fresh, Wet & Wild, Chico, October | sierranevada.com
Not long after hop harvest ends, Sierra Nevada taps breweries, including Drake's, 4 Hands, and Pizza Port, to make IPAs single-hopped, fresh-hopped, wet-hopped, and flavored with wild varieties.

COLORADO

Great American Beer Festival, Denver, October | greatamericanbeerfestival.com
The Alpha King Challenge—named after 3 Floyds' Alpha King Pale Ale and co-organized by hop supplier Yakima Chief–Hopunion—enlists brewers and beer writers to crown

"well-balanced and drinkable, yet highly-hopped ales" with a minimum of 60 IBUs. Past victors include Bell's Two Hearted Ale, Melvin Brewing 2x4, Russian River Pliny the Elder, and Port Brewing Hop-15. Montana's Überbrew won in 2015 for its black Double Tap Tactical IPA.

Southern Hemisphere Hop Festival, Denver, February | oskarblues.com
Inspired by Oskar Blues' newest year-round IPA, this festival tasks breweries, such as Odd13 and Ratio Beerworks, to make beers with Aussie and New Zealand hops.

JUL-IPA Festival, Boulder, July | thewestendtavern.com
Summer means celebrating IPAs of every stripe with hop-charged revelry, including Trinity, Odd13, Ska, and more expert practitioners.

FLORIDA

Dunedin Brewery IPA Festival, Dunedin, June | dunedinbrewery.com
The Sunshine State's oldest brewery joins forces with other standouts, including Green Bench and Funky Buddha, plus national experts, such as Ballast Point and Terrapin, in this hip, hip, hooray for all things IPA.

NEW YORK

Shmaltz Brewing Company IPA Festival, Clifton Park, January | shmaltzbrewing.com
This upstate brewery pours its IPAs, including the rye-driven Bittersweet Lenny's R.I.P.A., and selections from great Empire State breweries, such as Finback and Rushing Duck.

MISSOURI

Lupulin Carnival, St. Louis, April | lupulincarnival.com
Founded in 2012 by Four Hands, this big-top extravaganza features fire-breathers, acrobats, and a Ferris wheel to celebrate the annual release of the War Hammer Imperial IPA alongside scores of other Midwest IPAs.

OHIO

Celebration of the Hop, North Olmstead, October | fatheads.com
The annual Fat Head's hullabaloo enlists medal-winning Ohio breweries, such as Willoughby Brewing and Brew Kettle, plus heaps of IPAs from the host brewery.

Hopgeist, Cincinnati, October | rhinegeist.com
At its historic brewery in the Over-the-Rhine district, Rhinegeist pours its own double IPAs and those from brewers both regional (Seventh Son, MadTree, Jackie O's) and national, including California's Three Weavers and Cellarmaker.

OREGON

Saraveza II IPA Fest, Portland, August | saraveza.com
One of Portland's best beer shops and bars, Saraveza doles out at its yearly fest double IPAs from Gigantic, Oakshire, Block 15, and special house collaborations. Pair them with double bacon BLTs.

Hood River Hops Fest, Hood River, September | hoodriver.org/hops-fest

Since 2003, this shindig has highlighted the fresh-hop bounty of more than 40 local and regional brewers, including Double Mountain and Full Sail.

VERMONT

Hop Jam, Richmond, August | vthopjam.com

Based at the Bolton Valley Resort in the scenic Green Mountains, Hop Jam partners bands with a choice selection of Northeast-focused IPA breweries, such as Trillium, Treehouse, and Lost Nation.

VIRGINIA

IPA JAMBEEREE, Crozet, June | starrhill.com/ipa-jambeeree

Soak in views of the Blue Ridge Mountains while you soak up more than 50 Virginia IPAs from host Starr Hill and fellow Old Dominion brewers such as Blue Mountain, Champion, and Lickinghole Creek.

WASHINGTON

Fresh Hop Ale Festival, Yakima, October | freshhopalefestival.com

Most of America's hops grow in the Yakima Valley. Attend this festival for the freshest pale ales and IPAs that will ever pass your lips.

South Sound Beer Festival, Tacoma, November | washingtonbeer.com

Every fall, more than 30 Washington breweries, including Bale Breaker and Two Beers, join forces to pour around 100 terrific Pacific Northwest IPAs.

BELGIUM

Poperinge Beer and Hop Festival, September | hoppefeesten.be

Held triannually, the hop-championing get-together features a parade, the coronation of a hop queen, and Belgian beers that each contain at least 50 percent native hops.

SPAIN

Catalunya IPA Fest, Barcelona, February | facebook.com/mikkellerbarbarcelona

Mikkeller's Bar Barcelona spearheads this celebration of Spain's swell of great IPAs, capped by an awards ceremony.

GLOSSARY

Alcohol This by-product of fermentation occurs when yeasts devour sugars. Alcohol is measured in two categories: alcohol by volume (ABV) and alcohol by weight (ABW). In craft brewing, ABV is the standard measurement, but here's how to convert ABW to ABV: multiply by 1.25. The same volume of alcohol weighs about 80 percent as much as water, so a 4.8% ABW beer is about 6% ABV.

Ale One of two big families of beer (the other being lager). Like your great-aunt in Florida, ale yeasts favor warmer temperatures, hanging out at the top of the tank. Ale flavors and aromas are typically fruity and can taste sweeter and more full-bodied than lagers. Ales encompass an enormous grab bag of styles, including stouts, Belgian strong ales, and, yes, India pale ales.

Alpha acids Found in the hop cone, these contribute bitterness to beer. They're water-insoluble, but boiling them causes isomerization, which allows them to dissolve in water.

Aroma hops Hops used later in the boil for bouquet instead of bitterness.

Astringent A drying, puckering taste that's good or bad depending on your taste buds.

Barley The predominant cereal grain used to make beer. After water, the biggest ingredient in brewing.

Barrel The standard volume of measurement for brewing, which holds 31 gallons. A keg is half a barrel.

Beta acids Found in the hop cone, they primarily contribute to a beer's bouquet.

Bine A plant structure that allows a plant to climb by wrapping its stem around a support. Not to be confused with a vine, which climbs by means of tendrils or suckers.

Bittering hops Used early in the boil to add bitterness instead of aroma.

Boil The stage in brewing at which the wort boils in order to kill bacteria and yeast and cause proteins to coagulate. Hops are added during this stage.

Bottle-conditioned Beer carbonated naturally by live yeast in the bottle.

Brewers Association Based in Boulder, Colorado, this trade organization is America's preeminent craft beer group. They throw Denver's annual Great American Beer Festival.

Brew kettle The vessel in which the wort boils with hops.

Cascadian dark ale The name that Pacific Northwest brewers want to confer to dark, hoppy ales. The Beer Judge Certification Program recommends American-style black ale. I prefer the simpler black IPA. Whatever floats your boat.

Cask A wooden, metal, or plastic vessel used to mature, ferment, or flavor beer.

Craft brewer A nebulous, controversial, confusing term that, according to the Brewers Association, denotes a small, independent brewery that annually produces fewer than 6 millions barrels of traditional beer. Many microbreweries are no longer micro, so craft brewery is the preferred term—though artisanal and hand-crafted have diluted that phrase. An increasing number of breweries now prefer the adjective independent.

Double IPA A stronger, more intense IPA typically with a floor of 8% ABV. See imperial.

Dry-hopping Adding hops to beer that has finished fermenting or is conditioning. This step creates intense, fragrant aromatic brews.

Fermentation The metabolic process by which yeast consumes sugar, creating alcohol and carbon dioxide.

Filtration The removal of any floating proteins and yeasts that creates a clearer, more stable—and sometimes less flavorful—beer.

Fresh-hop beer A fragrant beer made with the year's first batches of dried hops. See wet-hop beer.

Gruit A medieval beer flavored with a mixture of herbs. Gruit predates the use of hops.

Great American Beer Festival The Super Bowl of American brewing since 1982. Hundreds of brewers enter the Denver competition to medal in nearly 80 categories and change their fortunes forever. That mile-high elevation ain't no joke!

Hopback A sealed, hops-stuffed vessel, between brew kettle and wort chiller, through which the wort circulates, snatching up heady aromas and flavors. Also called a hop jack.

Hop bursting An increasingly popular technique that adds massive amounts of hops during the end process of brewing, drawing out intense flavors and aromas but little bitterness.

Hop cannon A closed-loop dry-hopping technique in which hops are pressure-shot into the bottom of a tank, preventing the introduction of light and oxygen.

Hops The creeping bine Humulus lupulus, of which the female flowers (called cones) flavor beers and provide bitterness. Each variety has its own aroma or flavor profile.

Imperial IPA A stronger, more intense IPA, the phrase often used interchangeably with double IPA, but the ABV may reach double digits, putting it closer to triple territory.

India pale ale (IPA) A British-born, hop-focused style of beer that has become increasingly popular worldwide. The reason you bought or are reading this book.

International bitterness unit (IBU) A scientific measure of bitterness. Low IBU (Budweiser registers around 11) means the beer isn't hoppy. In triple digits, you're in for a mouth-scrunching ride. Not a perfect measure of perceived bitterness, however. A 5% ABV IPA with 50 IBUs will taste more intense than a 10% ABV IPA with 50 IBUs.

Lager The other main style of beer. Like penguins, bottom-fermenting lager yeasts prefer cooler temperatures. They also take longer to ferment (*lagern* means "to rest" in German). Lagers typically taste crisp, delicate, and as refreshing as a quick plunge in a cool lake in hot weather.

Malt Bathing cereal grains in water jump-starts germination, allowing the grain to create the enzymes required to convert starches and proteins into fermentable sugars. Heating and drying the grain halts the process. Like coffee, grain can be roasted to create different flavors and intensities.

Mash The initial step in brewing, in which crushed grain steeps in boiling water, transforming starches into sugars.

Mash tun The vessel in which brewers boil their mash.

Mouthfeel How beer subjectively feels when you drink it—a combination of body, texture, carbonation, and flavor.

Nanobrewery A pint-size brewery that runs on a three-barrel system or smaller.

Nitrogen tap A draft-beer system that courses nitrogen through beers, such as stouts, creating a creamy mouthfeel. Bottled and canned beers also can be nitrogenated.

Noble hops These aromatic, less bitter, European hop varieties, including Hallertauer, Tettnanger, Spalt, and Saaz, impart a spicy, herbal, zesty character. Commonly found in pilsners and European lagers.

Pasteurization Killing yeast by applying heat. Unpasteurized beers retain their yeast, which means the beer continues to evolve over time.

Pitch Adding yeast to the cooled-down wort.

Rye A cereal grain that imparts spiciness and a crisp character to beers and helps dry them out.

Session beer A beer low in alcohol, not in flavor, good for sipping during a long drinking session.

Skunked When UV light strikes beer, it causes a beer's isohumulones to break down, creating chemical compounds identical to those found in skunk spray. Never buy bottled beer shelved in a window.

Sparging Removing the grains from the mash, leaving behind hot, watery wort.

Triple IPA A great big IPA heaped with lots of hops. No hard-and-fast definition applies,

but a good rule of thumb is that triples start at 10% ABV.

Wet-hop beer A delicate, ephemeral fall specialty made with just-harvested hops not kilned or dried. It typically releases in September and October. See fresh-hop beer.

Wheat A grain that contributes smooth character, hazy hue, and light tartness.

Whirlpool hopping After flameout (when the boil ends) and during the whirlpool stage—in which centripetal force separates wort from coagulated proteins and hop matter—brewers add hops and allow them to isomerize slightly. The process adds flavor, aroma, and a little bit of bitterness.

Wild ale A catchall category of funky-tasting, offbeat beers dosed with wild yeast, such as *Brettanomyces*, and perhaps a souring bacteria, including *Lactobacillus* or *Pediococcus*.

World Beer Cup A high-status, biannual beer competition open to breweries worldwide.

Wort The hot soup extracted from the mash. It's an all-you-can-eat buffet for the yeast that creates beer.

Yeast The microscopic critters that eat sugar, create alcohol, and make beer o'clock the best time of day. Each strain provides a different flavor profile, and breweries often develop their own strains.

BEER CHECKLIST

- [ ] 3 Floyds Dreadnaught (USA)
- [ ] 4 Pines Fresh in Season IPA (AUSTRALIA)
- [ ] 8 Wired Tall Poppy (NZ)
- [ ] 21st Amendment Toaster Pastry (USA)
- [ ] Alchemist Heady Topper (USA)
- [ ] AleSmith IPA (USA)
- [ ] Allagash Hugh Malone (USA)
- [ ] Alltech Lexington Kentucky Rye Barrel IPA (USA)
- [ ] Almanac IPA (USA)
- [ ] Almond '22 Pink IPA (ITALY)
- [ ] Alpine Duet (USA)
- [ ] Amager Bryghus / Surly Todd the Axe Man (DENMARK)
- [ ] Anchorage Galaxy White IPA (USA)
- [ ] Arizona Wilderness Refuge IPA (USA)
- [ ] Art Cervesers Art La Indiana (SPAIN)
- [ ] Avery IPA (USA)
- [ ] Baird The Fruitful Life Citrus IPA (JAPAN)
- [ ] Bale Breaker Topcutter IPA (USA)
- [ ] Ballast Point Sculpin (USA)
- [ ] Barley Brown's Pallet Jack IPA (USA)
- [ ] Base Camp In-Tents IPL (USA)
- [ ] Beachwood Amalgamator (USA)
- [ ] Beanery Coffee IPA (USA)
- [ ] Bear Republic Hop Rod Rye (USA)
- [ ] Beavertown Black Betty (UK)
- [ ] Beer Here Dark Hops (DENMARK)
- [ ] Bell's Two Hearted Ale (USA)
- [ ] Bellwoods Witchshark Imperial IPA (CANADA)
- [ ] Bissell Brothers Substance Ale (USA)
- [ ] Black Market Seek and Destroy (USA)
- [ ] Bodebrown Cacau IPA (BRAZIL)
- [ ] Boneyard RPM IPA (USA)
- [ ] Boulevard 80-Acre Hoppy Wheat Beer (USA)
- [ ] Brasserie de la Senne Taras Boulba (BELGIUM)
- [ ] Brasserie Dunham Tropicale IPA (CANADA)
- [ ] Brasseurs du Grand Paris IPA Citra Galactique (FRANCE)
- [ ] Breakside IPA (USA)
- [ ] Brew by Numbers Session IPA (UK)
- [ ] Brew Kettle White Raja (USA)
- [ ] BrewDog Jack Hammer (UK)
- [ ] BrewFist 2Late (ITALY)
- [ ] Brewski Mangofebeer (SWEDEN)
- [ ] Brooklyn East IPA (USA)
- [ ] Brussels Beer Project Delta (BELGIUM)
- [ ] Buxton Axe Edge (UK)
- [ ] Ca l'Arenys Guineu Riner (SPAIN)
- [ ] Camden Town IHL (UK)
- [ ] Carton Boat Beer (USA)
- [ ] Castor Yakima IPA (CANADA)
- [ ] Cellarmaker Dank Williams (USA)
- [ ] Central City Red Betty Imperial IPA (CANADA)

- ☐ Champion Missile IPA (USA)
- ☐ Chorlton Amarillo Sour (UK)
- ☐ Cigar City Jai Alai IPA (USA)
- ☐ Cloudwater U.S. Light Ales and Session IPAs (UK)
- ☐ Columbus Bodhi (USA)
- ☐ Comrade Superpower IPA (USA)
- ☐ COOP F5 IPA (USA)
- ☐ Coronado Islander IPA (USA)
- ☐ Creature Comforts Tropicália (USA)
- ☐ Crooked Stave Hop Savant (USA)
- ☐ Cucapà Runaway IPA (MEXICO)
- ☐ La Cumbre Elevated IPA (USA)
- ☐ Dad & Dudes Sativa IPA (USA)
- ☐ Dark Horse Double Crooked Tree (USA)
- ☐ DC Brau On the Wings of Armageddon (USA)
- ☐ De Ranke XX Bitter (BELGIUM)
- ☐ Deep Ellum IPA (USA)
- ☐ Del Borgo My Antonia (ITALY)
- ☐ Denver Incredible Pedal IPA (USA)
- ☐ Deschutes Chasin' Freshies (USA)
- ☐ Dieu du Ciel! Dernière Volonté (CANADA)
- ☐ Dogfish Head 120 Minute IPA (USA)
- ☐ Driftwood Sartori Harvest IPA (CANADA)
- ☐ Ecliptic Orbiter IPA (USA)
- ☐ Edge Taronja HoRyezon Rye IPA (SPAIN)
- ☐ Elav Techno Double IPA (ITALY)
- ☐ Elysian Avatar Jasmine IPA (USA)
- ☐ Emelisse Triple IPA (NETHERLANDS)
- ☐ Epic Escape to Colorado (USA)
- ☐ Epic Hop Zombie (NZ)
- ☐ Evil Twin Molotov Cocktail Heavy (USA)
- ☐ Fat Head's Hop JuJu Imperial IPA (USA)

- ☐ Feral Barrel Fermented Hog (AUSTRALIA)
- ☐ Fiddlehead Second Fiddle (USA)
- ☐ Firestone Walker Wookey Jack (USA)
- ☐ Foothills Jade (USA)
- ☐ Fort George Java the Hop (USA)
- ☐ Foundation Epiphany (USA)
- ☐ Founders All Day IPA (USA)
- ☐ Four Peaks Hop Knot (USA)
- ☐ Four Winds Juxtapose IPA (CANADA)
- ☐ Fuller's IPA (UK)
- ☐ Garage IPA (SPAIN)
- ☐ Garage Project Death from Above (NZ)
- ☐ Gigantic IPA (USA)
- ☐ Good People Snake Handler (USA)
- ☐ Goose Island IPA (USA)
- ☐ Great Divide Titan IPA (USA)
- ☐ Great Lakes Commodore Perry (USA)
- ☐ Great Lakes THRUST! (CANADA)
- ☐ Great Leap Ghost General Wheat IPA (CHINA)
- ☐ Green Flash Green Bullet (USA)
- ☐ Grey Sail Captain's Daughter (USA)
- ☐ Grimm Artisanal Super Going (USA)
- ☐ Guinness Nitro IPA (IRELAND)
- ☐ Half Acre GoneAway (USA)
- ☐ Hardywood Park Hoplar (USA)
- ☐ Harpoon Take 5 (USA)
- ☐ Hill Farmstead Susan (USA)
- ☐ Hof Ten Dormaal Politician (BELGIUM)
- ☐ Hong Kong Big Wave Bay (CHINA)
- ☐ Hops & Grain A Pale Mosaic (USA)
- ☐ Hopworks IPA (USA)
- ☐ Insurgente Nocturna (MEXICO)

- [ ] Ithaca Flower Power (USA)
- [ ] Jack's Abby Hoponius Union (USA)
- [ ] Jailbreak Welcome to Scoville (USA)
- [ ] Kaiju! Where Strides the Behemoth (AUSTRALIA)
- [ ] Karl Strauss Mosaic Session Ale (USA)
- [ ] Kern River Just Outstanding (USA)
- [ ] Kernel IPA (UK)
- [ ] Kiuchi Hitachino Nest Japanese Classic Ale (JAPAN)
- [ ] Knee Deep Hop-De-Ranged (USA)
- [ ] Lagunitas A Little Sumpin' Sumpin' Ale (USA)
- [ ] Lawson's Finest Liquids Sip of Sunshine (USA)
- [ ] Left Hand Warrior IPA (USA)
- [ ] Lervig Rye IPA (NORWAY)
- [ ] Liberty Yakima Scarlet (NZ)
- [ ] Lone Pint Yellow Rose (USA)
- [ ] Magic Rock Cannonball (UK)
- [ ] Maine Lunch (USA)
- [ ] Marble IPA (USA)
- [ ] Master Gao Baby IPA (CHINA)
- [ ] Matt Saranac Gen IV Session IPA (USA)
- [ ] Meantime IPA (UK)
- [ ] Melvin 2x4 DIPA (USA)
- [ ] Mike Hess Habitus Rye IPA (USA)
- [ ] Mikkeller Not Just Another Wit (DENMARK)
- [ ] Modern Times Fortunate Islands (USA)
- [ ] Modus Operandi Former Tenant Red IPA (AUSTRALIA)
- [ ] Moody Tongue Sliced Nectarine IPA (USA)
- [ ] Moor Hoppiness (UK)

- [ ] Moylan's Hop Craic XXXXIPA (USA)
- [ ] Naparbier HopDoom (SPAIN)
- [ ] Nebraska HopAnomaly (USA)
- [ ] New Belgium Le Terroir (USA)
- [ ] New England G-Bot (USA)
- [ ] Ninkasi Total Domination (USA)
- [ ] NoDa Hop, Drop, 'n' Roll (USA)
- [ ] North Peak Vicious American Wheat IPA (USA)
- [ ] Notch Left of the Dial (USA)
- [ ] Odd13 Codename: Superfan (USA)
- [ ] Odell IPA (USA)
- [ ] Omnipollo Nebuchadnezzar Imperial IPA (SWEDEN)
- [ ] Oskar Blues Pinner Throwback IPA (USA)
- [ ] Other Half All Green Everything (USA)
- [ ] Otter Creek Fresh Slice (USA)
- [ ] Pabst Ballantine IPA (USA)
- [ ] Pit-Caribou Brett Session IPA (CANADA)
- [ ] Pizza Boy Eternal Sunshine (USA)
- [ ] Port City Monumental IPA (USA)
- [ ] Port Hop-15 (USA)
- [ ] Reuben's Crikey IPA (USA)
- [ ] Revolution Anti-Hero IPA (USA)
- [ ] Rhinegeist Truth (USA)
- [ ] Rothhammer Nazca (CHILE)
- [ ] Russian River Pliny the Elder (USA)
- [ ] Saint Louis Schlafly Tasmanian IPA (USA)
- [ ] Samuel Adams Rebel Raw (USA)
- [ ] SanTan Brewing MoonJuice IPA (USA)
- [ ] Short's Juicy Tree (USA)

- [ ] Sierra Nevada Harvest Wet Hop IPA—Northern Hemisphere (USA)
- [ ] Sigtuna East River Lager (SWEDEN)
- [ ] Siren Liquid Mistress (UK)
- [ ] Ska Modus Hoperandi (USA)
- [ ] Smuttynose Rhye IPA (USA)
- [ ] Snake River Pako's IPA (USA)
- [ ] Societe The Pupil (USA)
- [ ] Southern Prohibition Mississippi Fire Ant (USA)
- [ ] Southern Tier Tangier (USA)
- [ ] Spiteful IPA (USA)
- [ ] Stone Go To IPA (USA)
- [ ] Stoneface IPA (USA)
- [ ] Summit Horizon Red IPA (USA)
- [ ] Surly Furious (USA)
- [ ] SweetWater IPA (USA)
- [ ] Terrapin Hopsecutioner (USA)
- [ ] Thornbridge Halcyon (UK)
- [ ] Tiny Rebel Hadouken (UK)
- [ ] To Øl Black Malts & Body Salts Black Coffee IIPA (DENMARK)
- [ ] Toccalmatto B Space Invader (ITALY)
- [ ] Toppling Goliath King Sue (USA)
- [ ] Town Hall Masala Mama IPA (USA)

- [ ] Tree House Green (USA)
- [ ] Trillium Congress Street (USA)
- [ ] Trinity Red Swingline IPA Primitif (USA)
- [ ] Troëgs Nugget Nectar (USA)
- [ ] Tupiniquim Polimango (BRAZIL)
- [ ] Twisted Pine Roots Revival Carrot IPA (USA)
- [ ] Two Brothers Heavy Handed Wet Hop IPA (USA)
- [ ] Two Roads Lil' Heaven (USA)
- [ ] Uinta Trader Session IPA (USA)
- [ ] Unfiltered Double Orange Ale (CANADA)
- [ ] Upland Campside Session IPA (USA)
- [ ] Upslope Thai Style White IPA (USA)
- [ ] Victory DirtWolf (USA)
- [ ] Vivant Triomphe Belgian Style IPA (USA)
- [ ] Way Double APA (BRAZIL)
- [ ] Weird Beard Out of Office (UK)
- [ ] Westbrook IPA (USA)
- [ ] Wicked Weed Pernicious (USA)
- [ ] Widmer Brothers Upheaval IPA (USA)
- [ ] Wild Beer Company Evolver IPA (UK)
- [ ] Wormtown Be Hoppy (USA)
- [ ] Worthington's White Shield (UK)

INDEX